The Elements
AIR

JUSTYN TIME

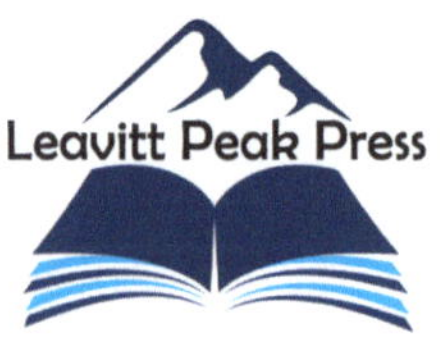

ISBN: 978-1-962363-35-8 (sc)
ISBN: 978-1-962363-36-5 (e)

Rev. date: 12/07/2023

Introduction

The five Elements are Aether, Air, Earth, Fire and Water. These are the Elements that exist within our reality. Of these five elements four are physical and the fith, Aether, is also referred to as spiritual. It is the authors opinion that all of the physical elements are contolled and or manipulated by the Aether or spirit world. This thought process is predicated upon the theory that all of the Elements have patterns within themslves. Patterns that when closely observed can be documented photographically. This series, Justyn Time / The Elements, showcases the patterns and designs within each of them. The Author challenges you to study the images within to discover the magical realm that lies within each or the Elements. Air is considered a Pure element.

We need to understand that the air around us is made up of a variety of gasses, primarily nitrogen and oxygen with almost 1% of argon and even smaller amounts of carbon dioxide and other elements such as krypton and helium. The composition of air is just right for life on earth. the excerpt is from learning/center.homeschool science tools.com/article/four-elements.

He first started seeing images in the clouds in April or May of the Year 2020. They were very faint, hardly noticeable images within the clouds. The first visions were seen on the above the football field above at Willow Glen High School, home of the Rams. Since that day I've used the following cameras to document and capture the artwork in the skies, the air element.

Sony a7c, Canon 70D, Apple iPhone 11 / 13

The iPhone has been the go to camera due to the ability to capture, enhance and post to social media. The second reason is the ease of use and functionality of the panoramic option. Over the last 3 years the images have been very unique and multi-layered. The imagery within each cloud configuration is so unique that when you rotate the image 90° counterclockwise, you will see a different image revealed. Truly the heavens declare the glory of God! Our God is able to create such magnificent and unique imagery in the skies above us.

This truly gives us the best reason to stop and look up. the scripture I quoted earlier is Psalm 19:1 the heavens declare the almighty of God and the firmament showeth his handiwork. Acts 2:17 reads in the last days God says I will pour out my spirit on all kinds of people your sons and daughters will prophesy your young men will see visions your old men will dream dreams. We are definitely in the last days as prophesied in the Bible.

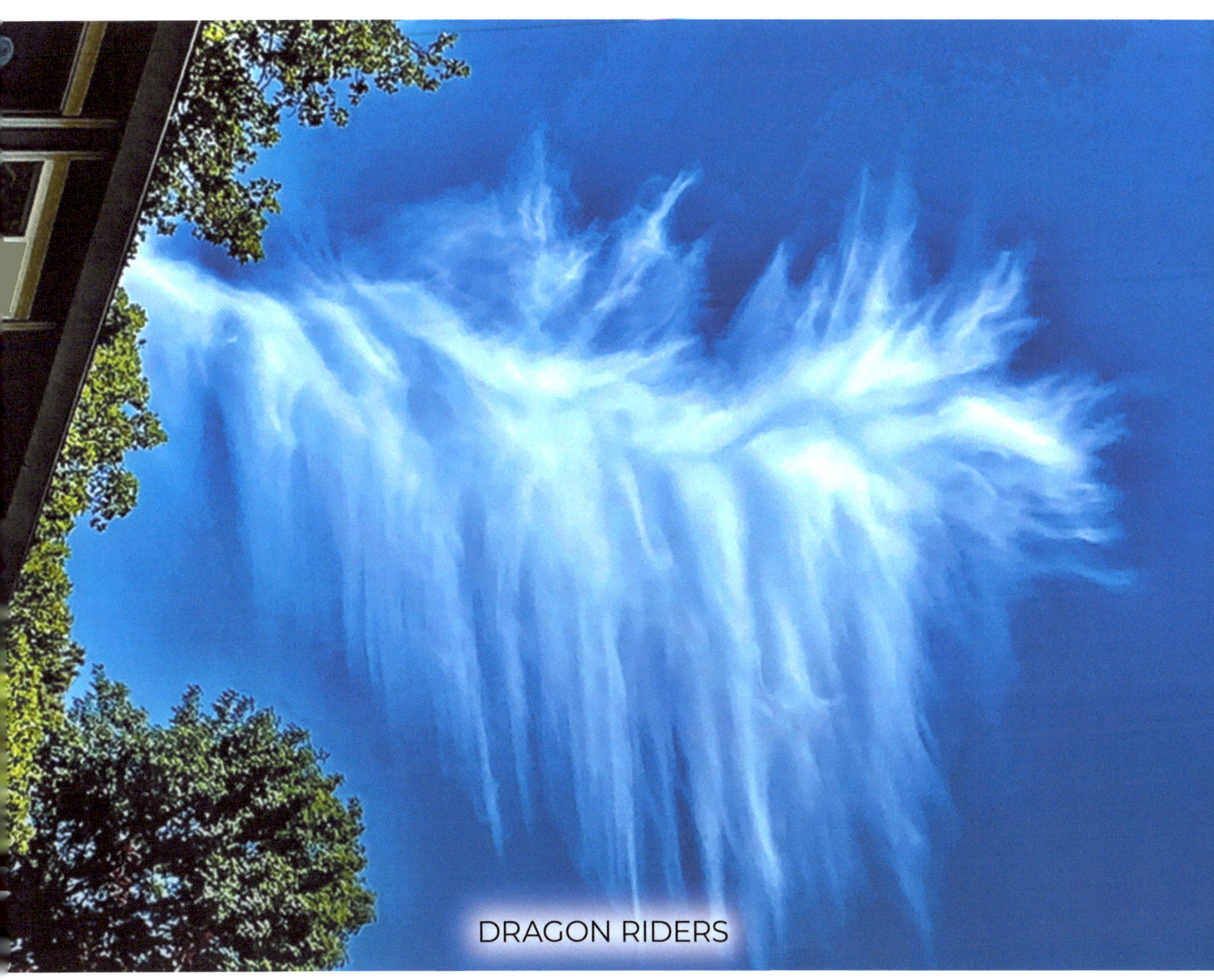

DRAGON RIDERS

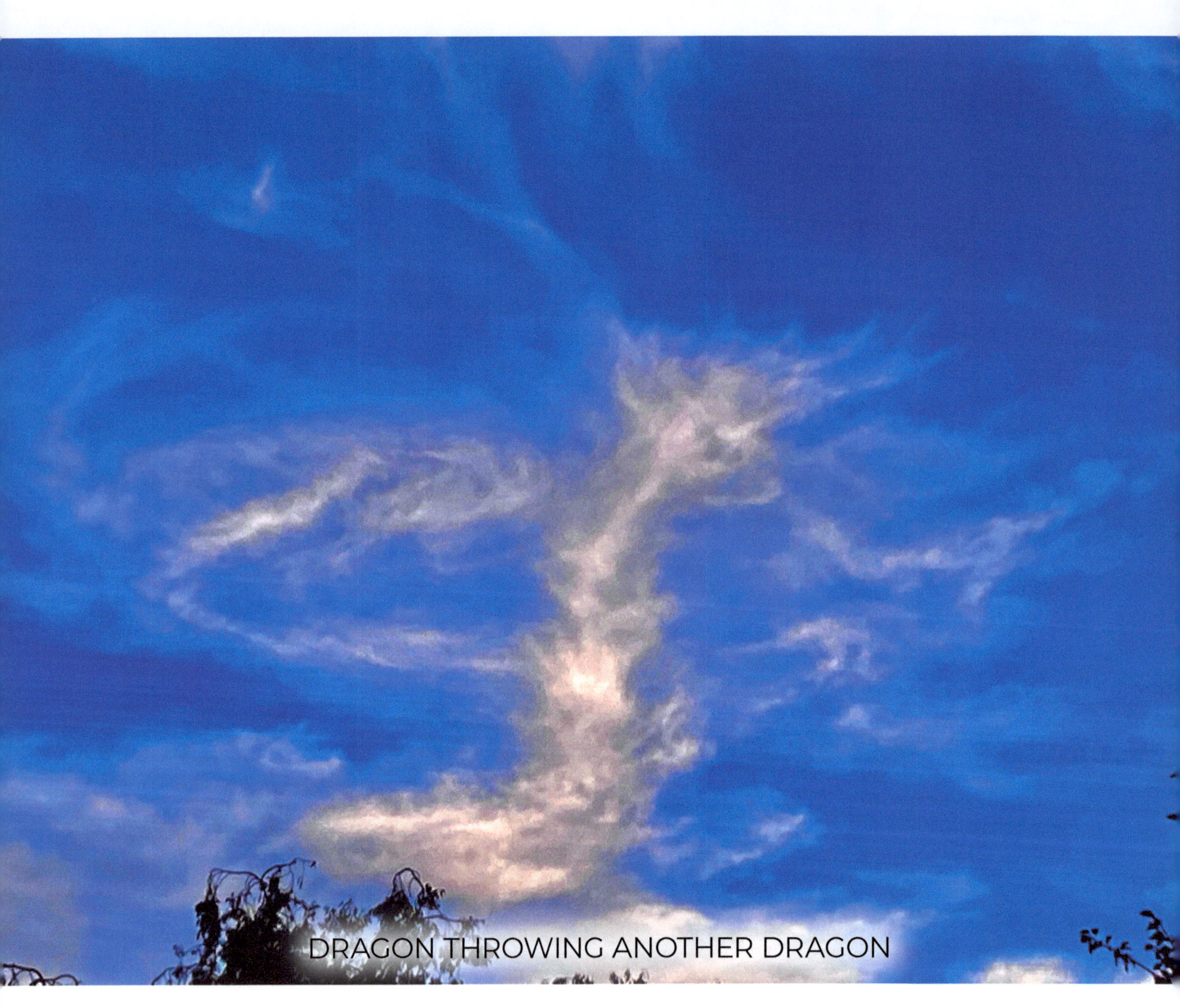

DRAGON THROWING ANOTHER DRAGON

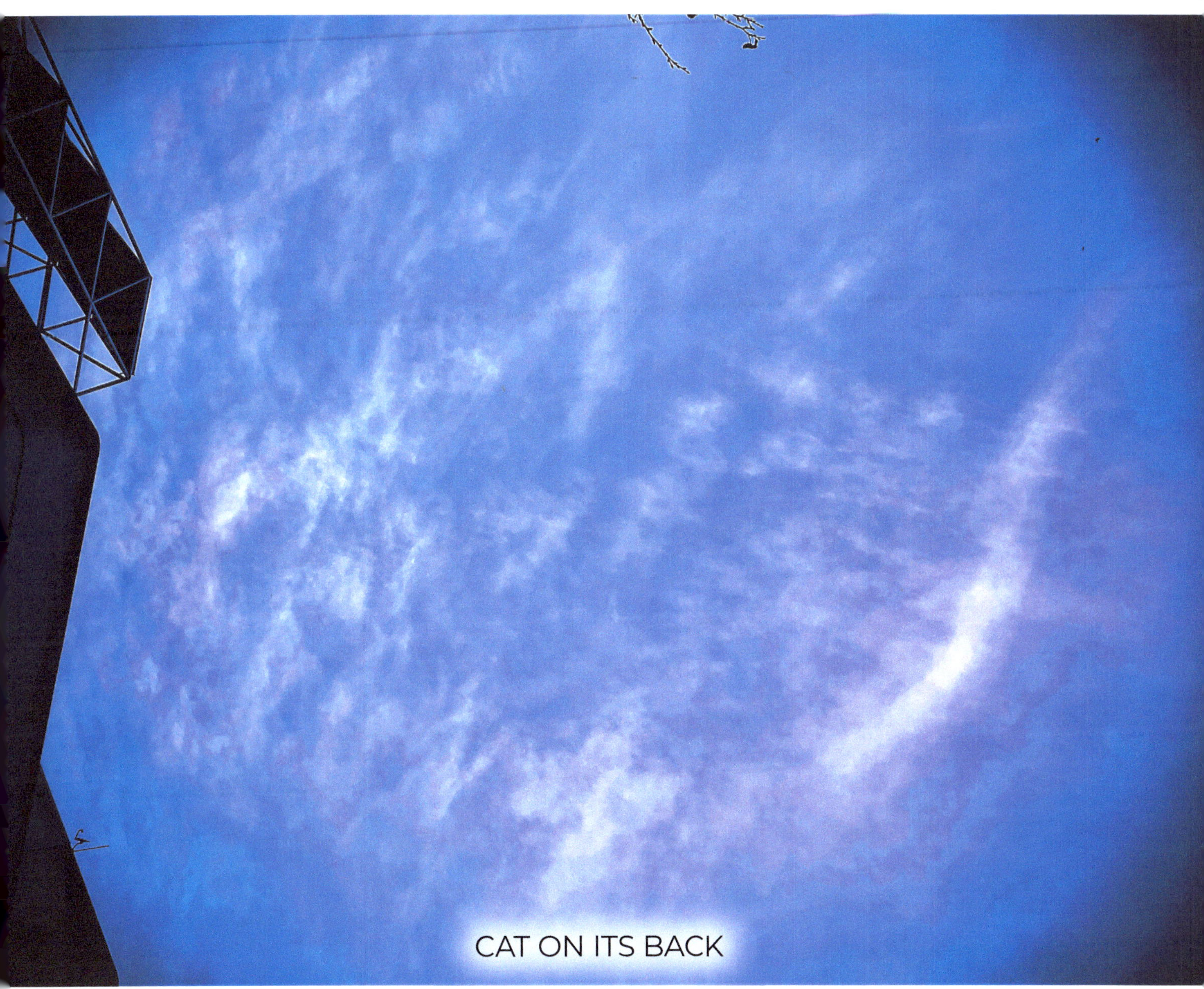

CAT ON ITS BACK

DRAGONFLY

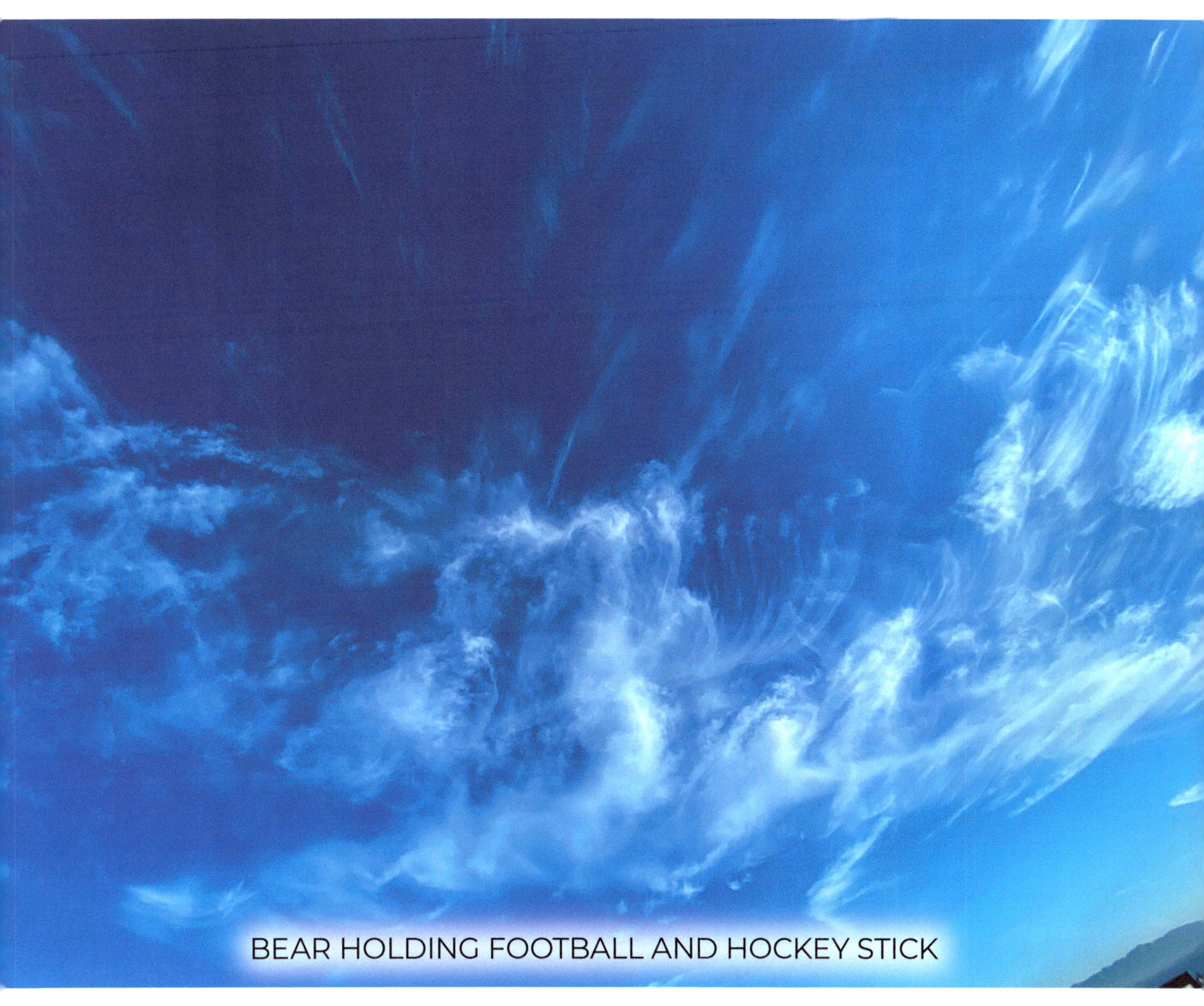

BEAR HOLDING FOOTBALL AND HOCKEY STICK

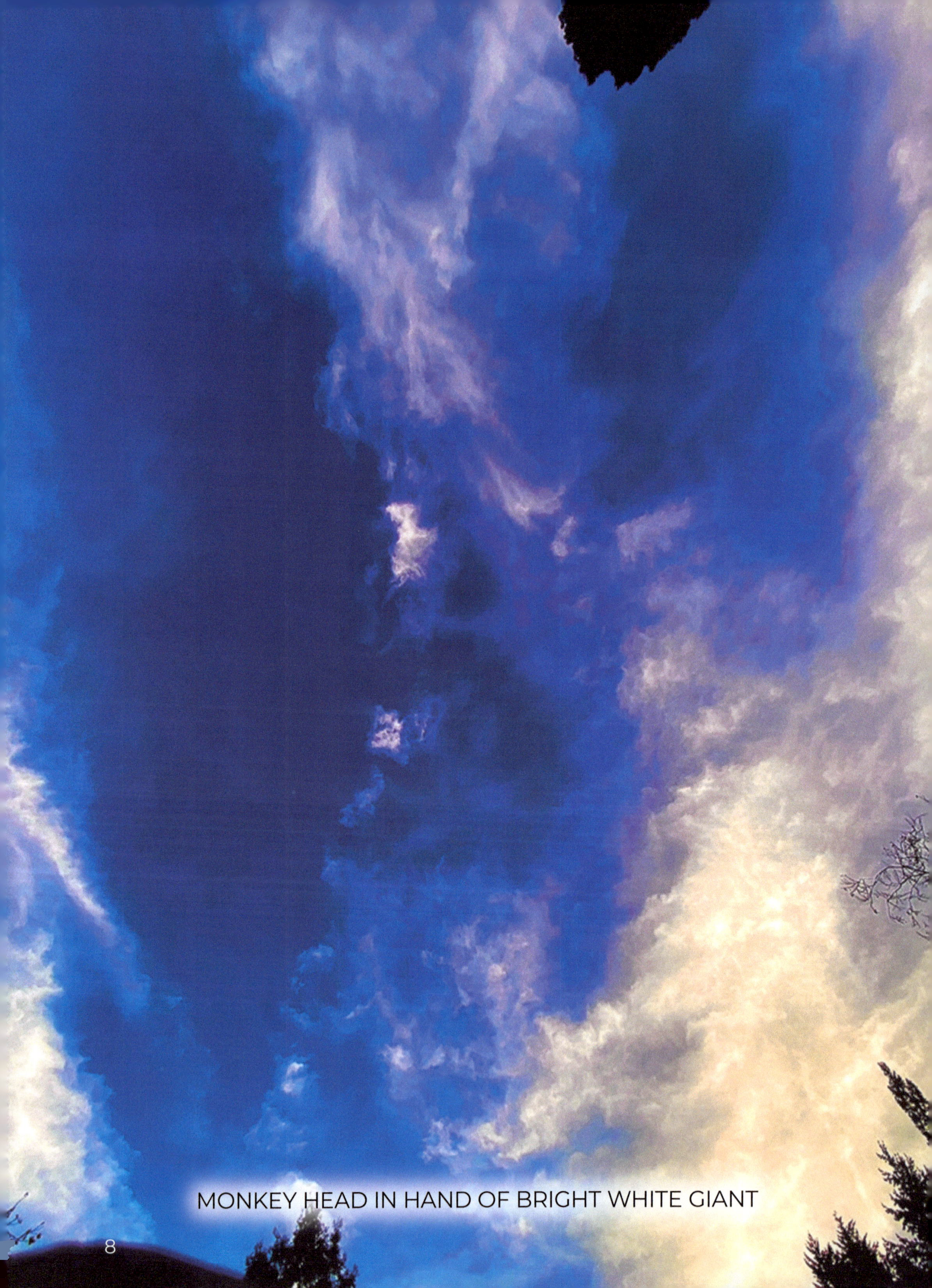

MONKEY HEAD IN HAND OF BRIGHT WHITE GIANT

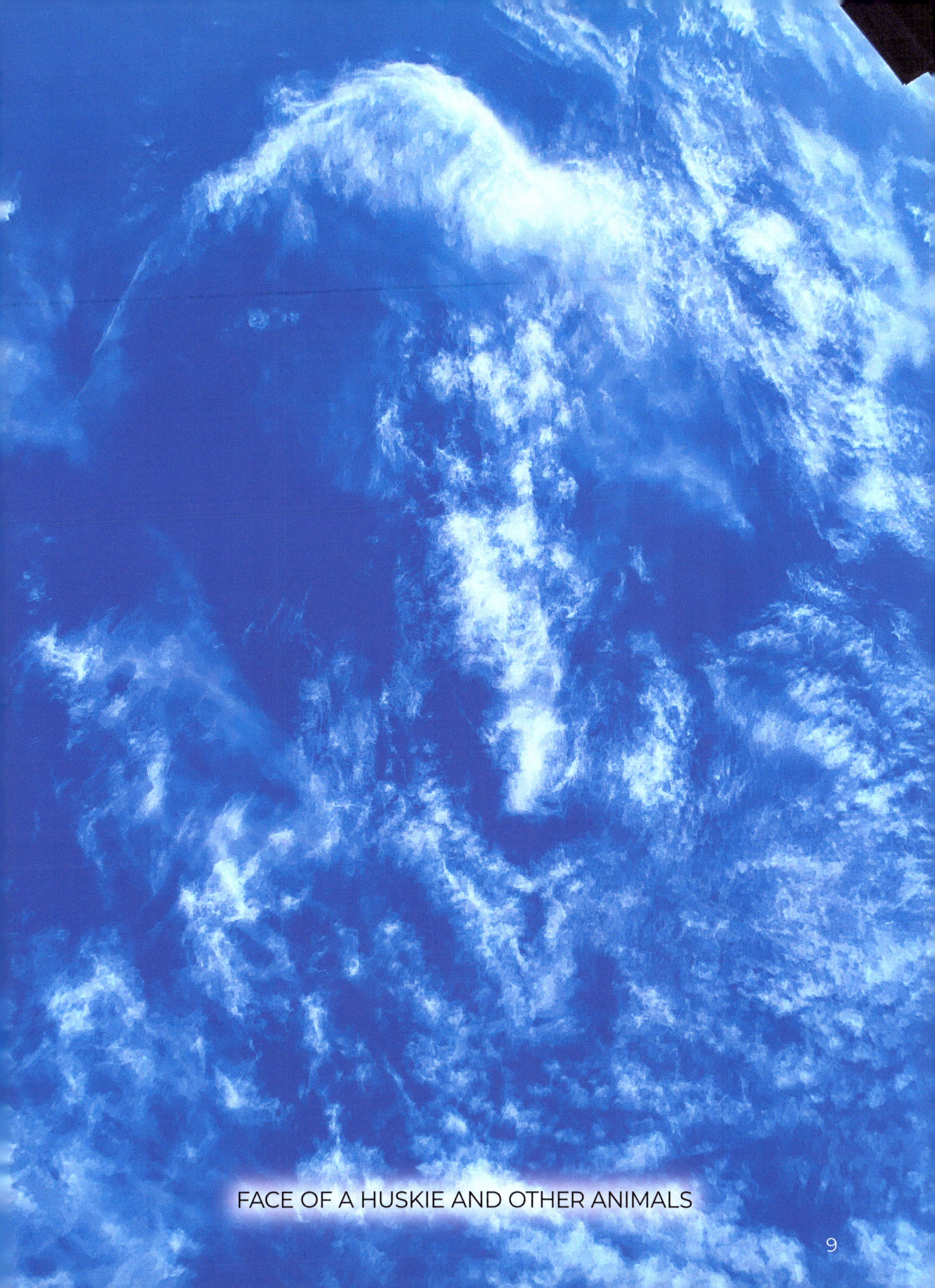

FACE OF A HUSKIE AND OTHER ANIMALS

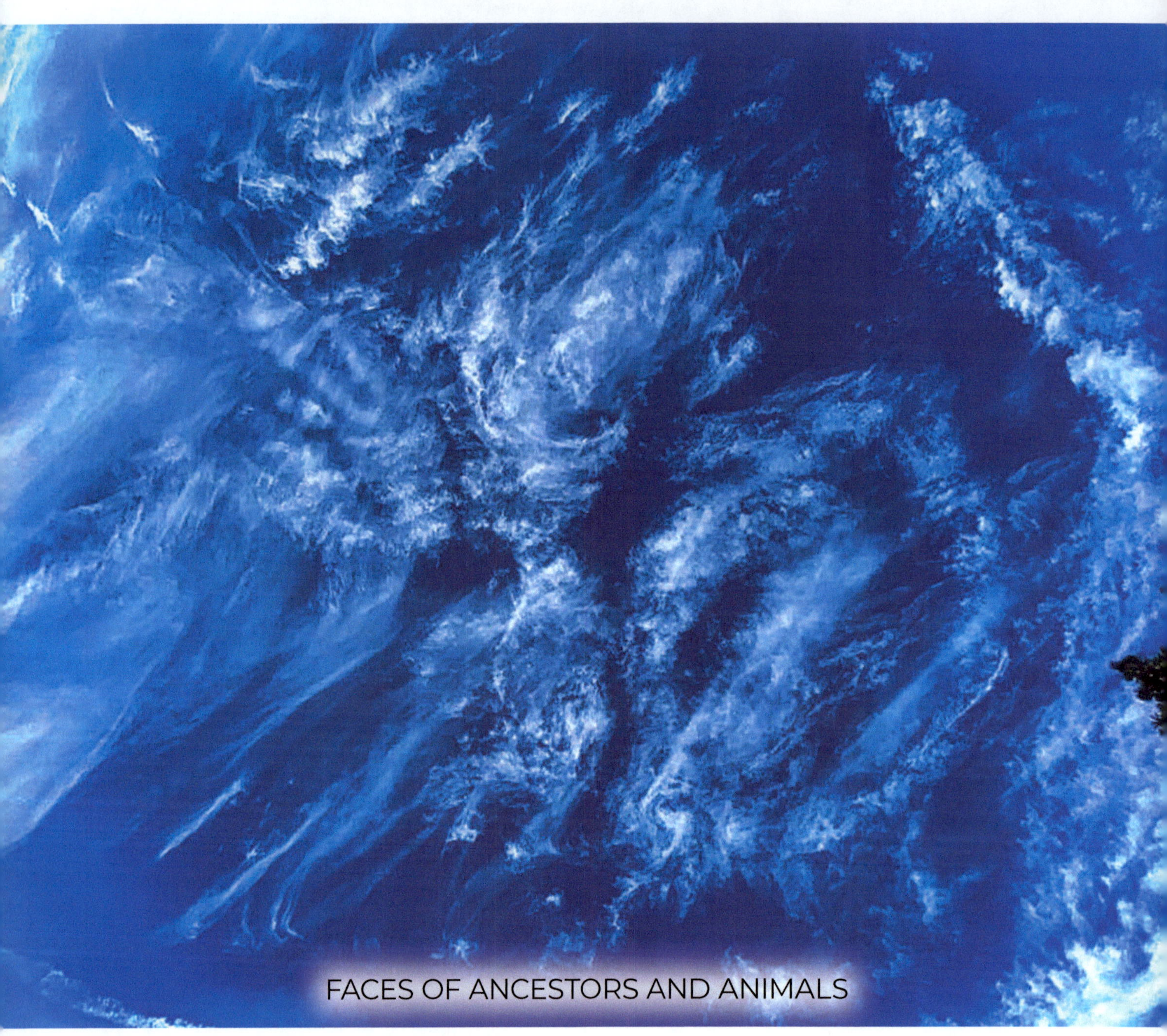

FACES OF ANCESTORS AND ANIMALS

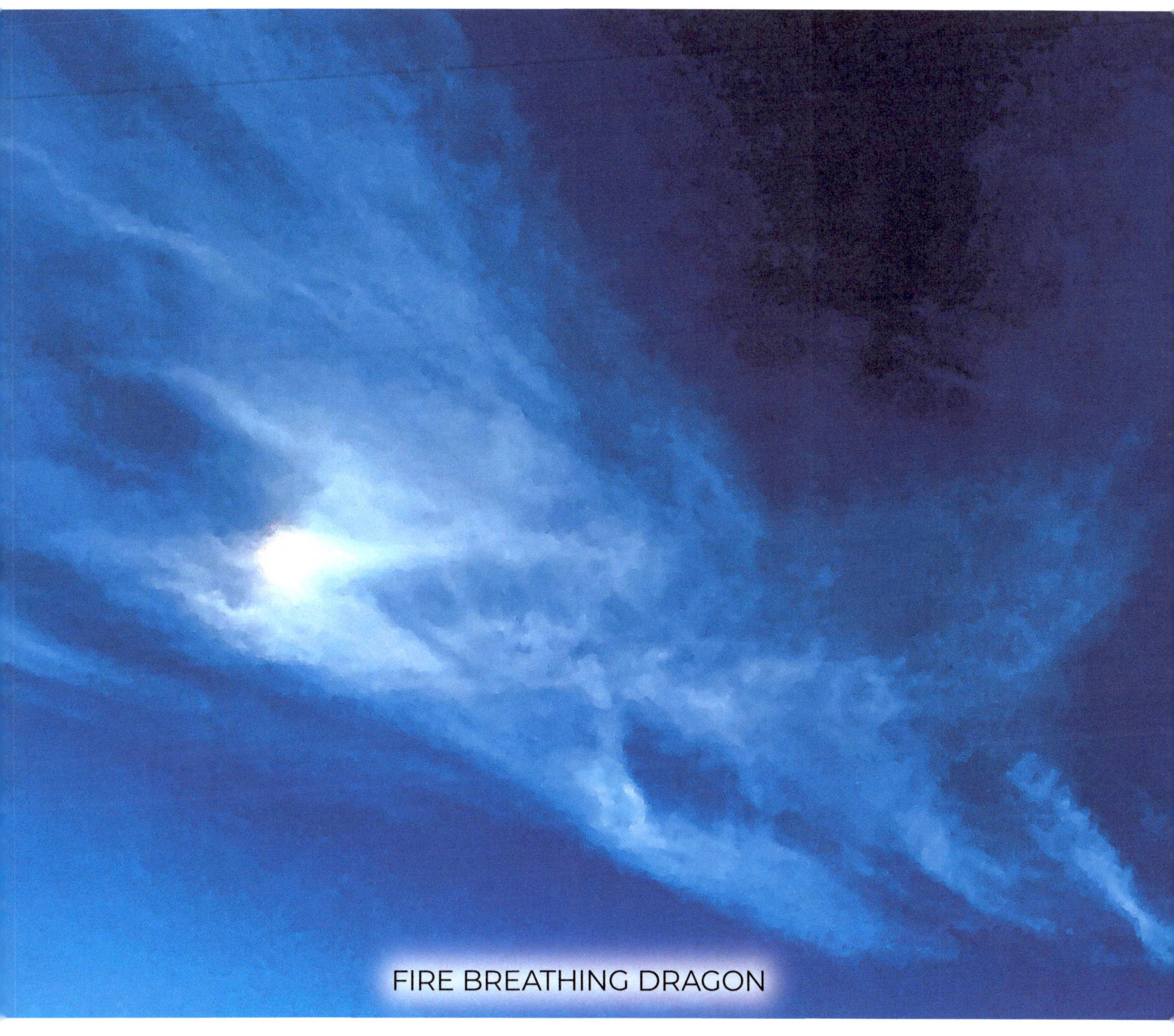

FIRE BREATHING DRAGON

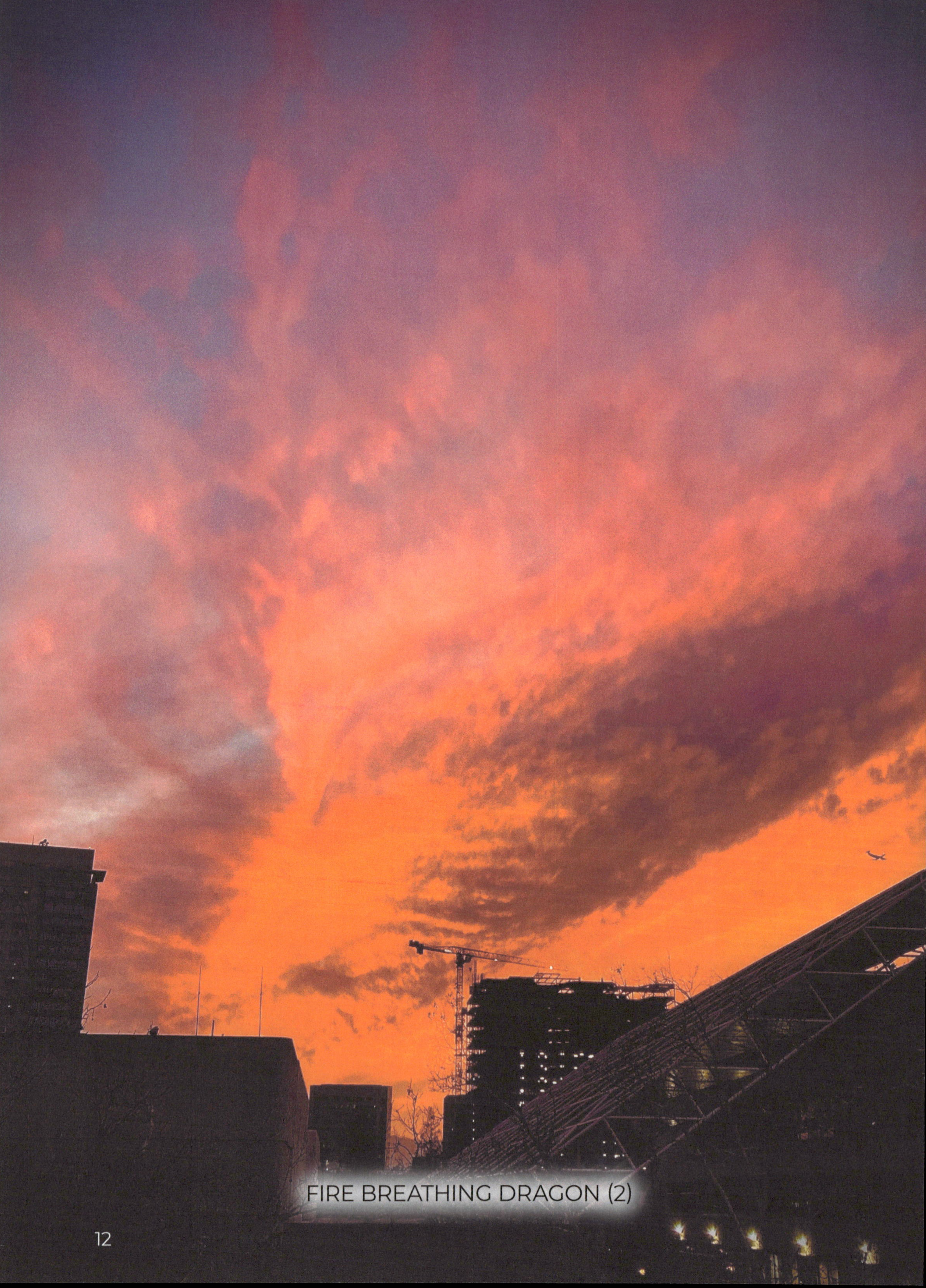

FIRE BREATHING DRAGON (2)

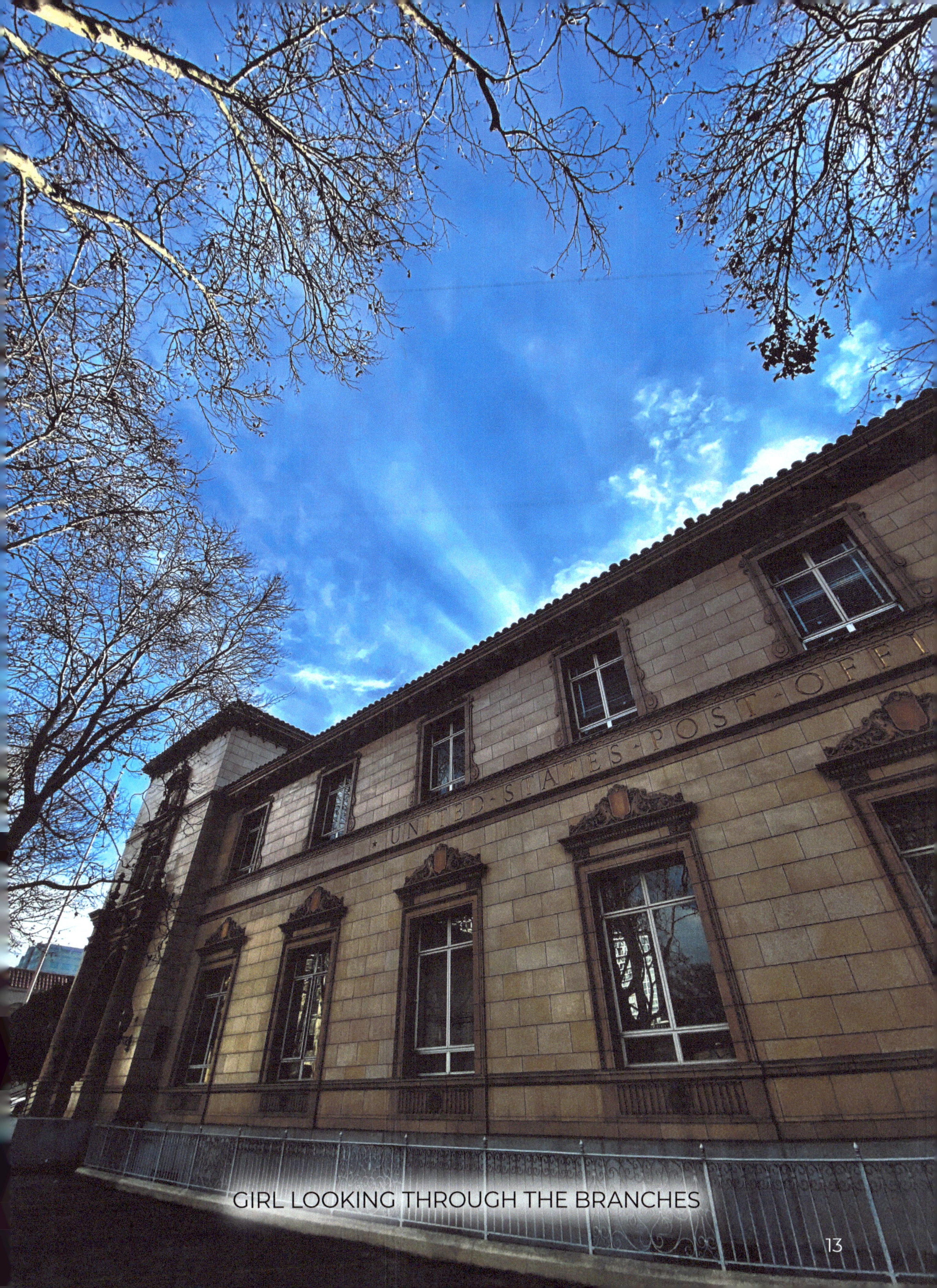

GIRL LOOKING THROUGH THE BRANCHES

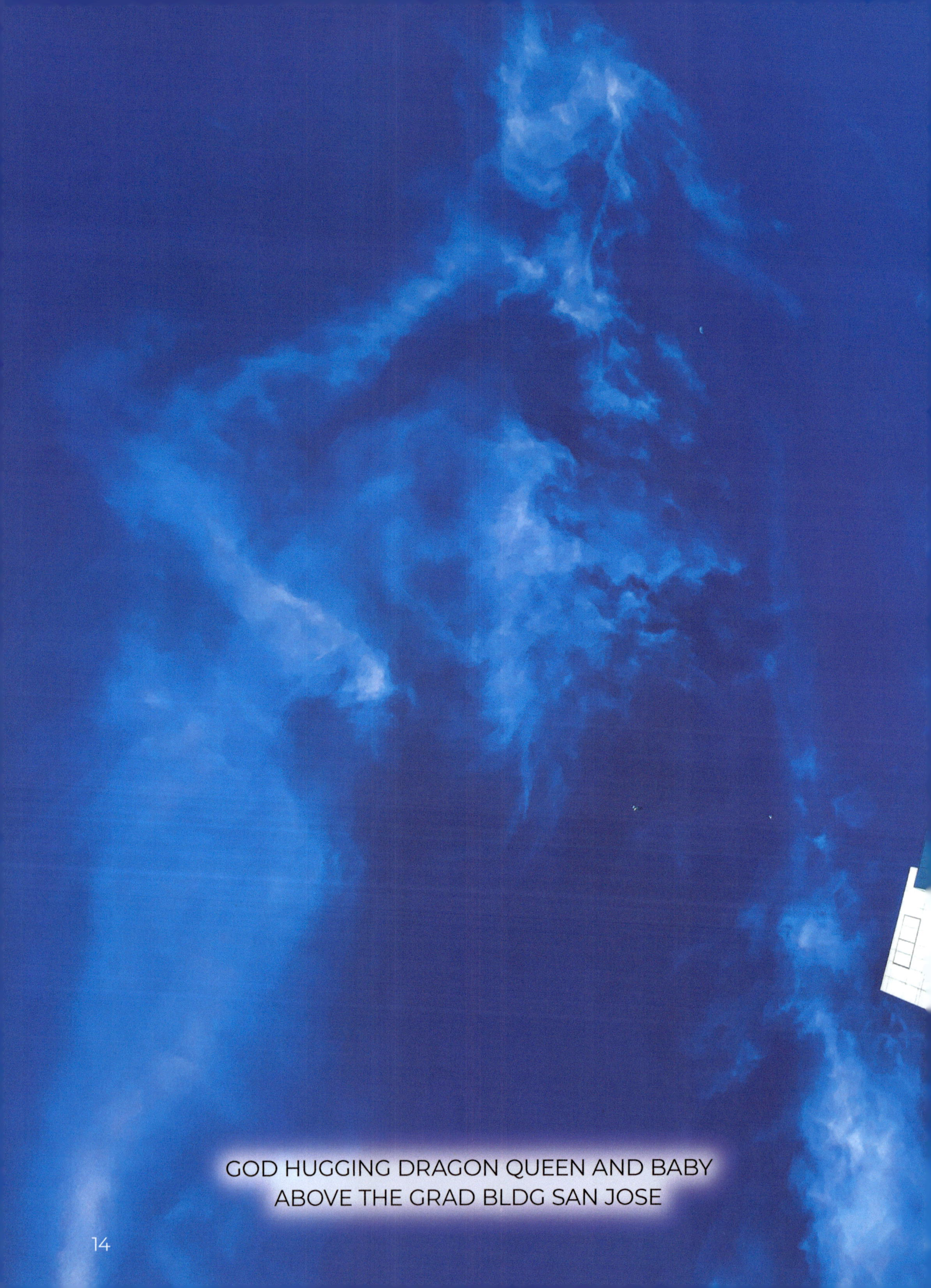

GOD HUGGING DRAGON QUEEN AND BABY
ABOVE THE GRAD BLDG SAN JOSE

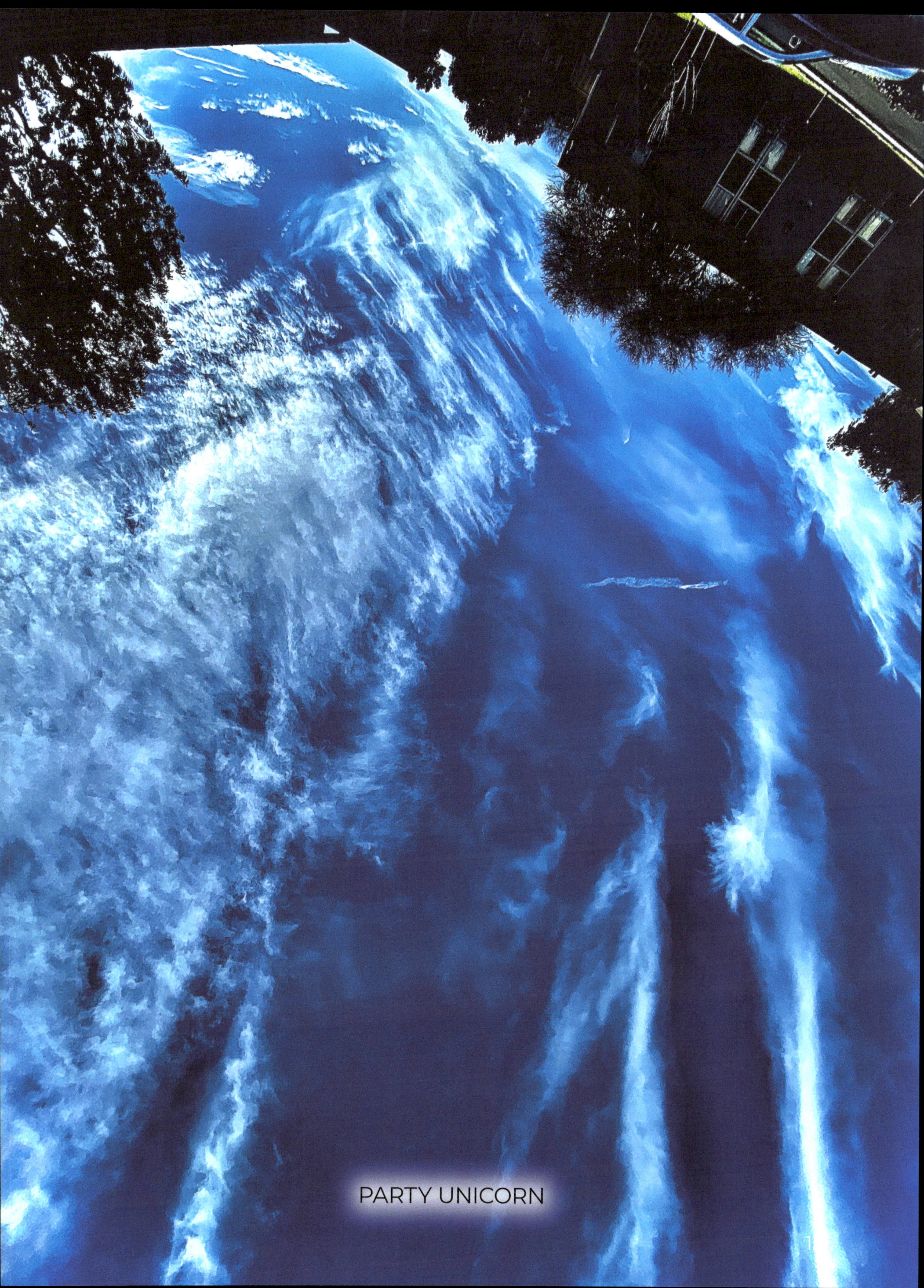
PARTY UNICORN

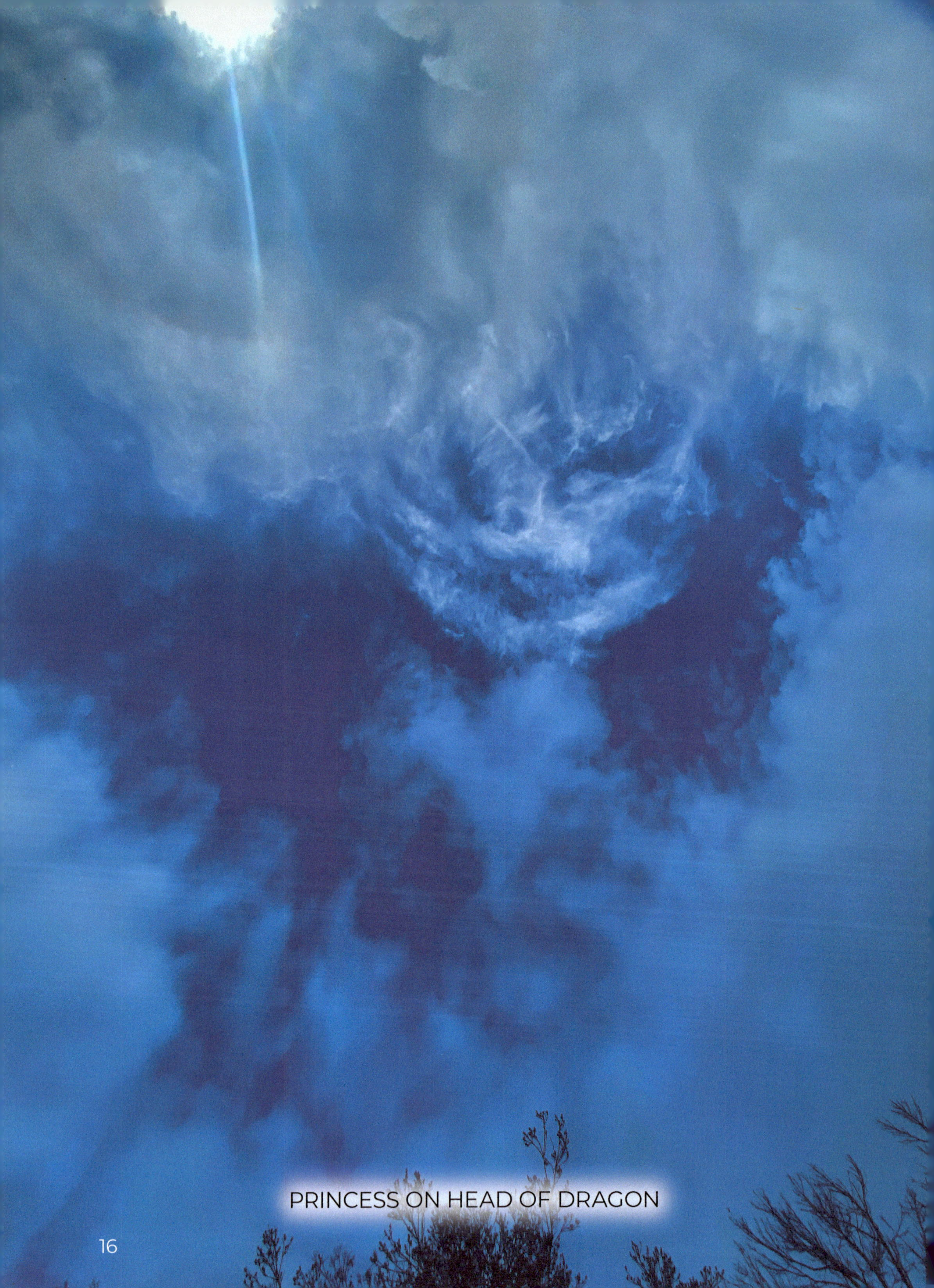

PRINCESS ON HEAD OF DRAGON

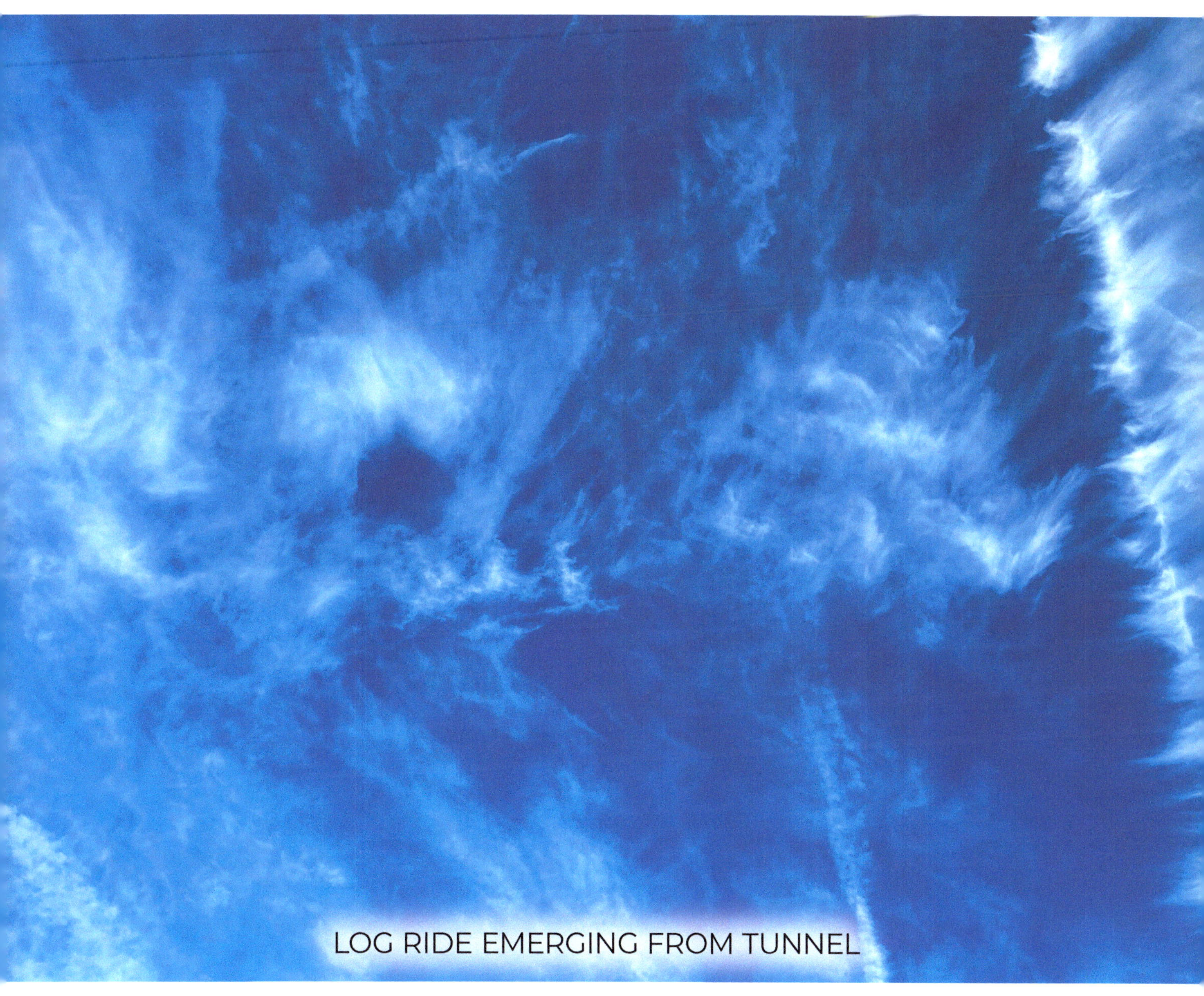

LOG RIDE EMERGING FROM TUNNEL

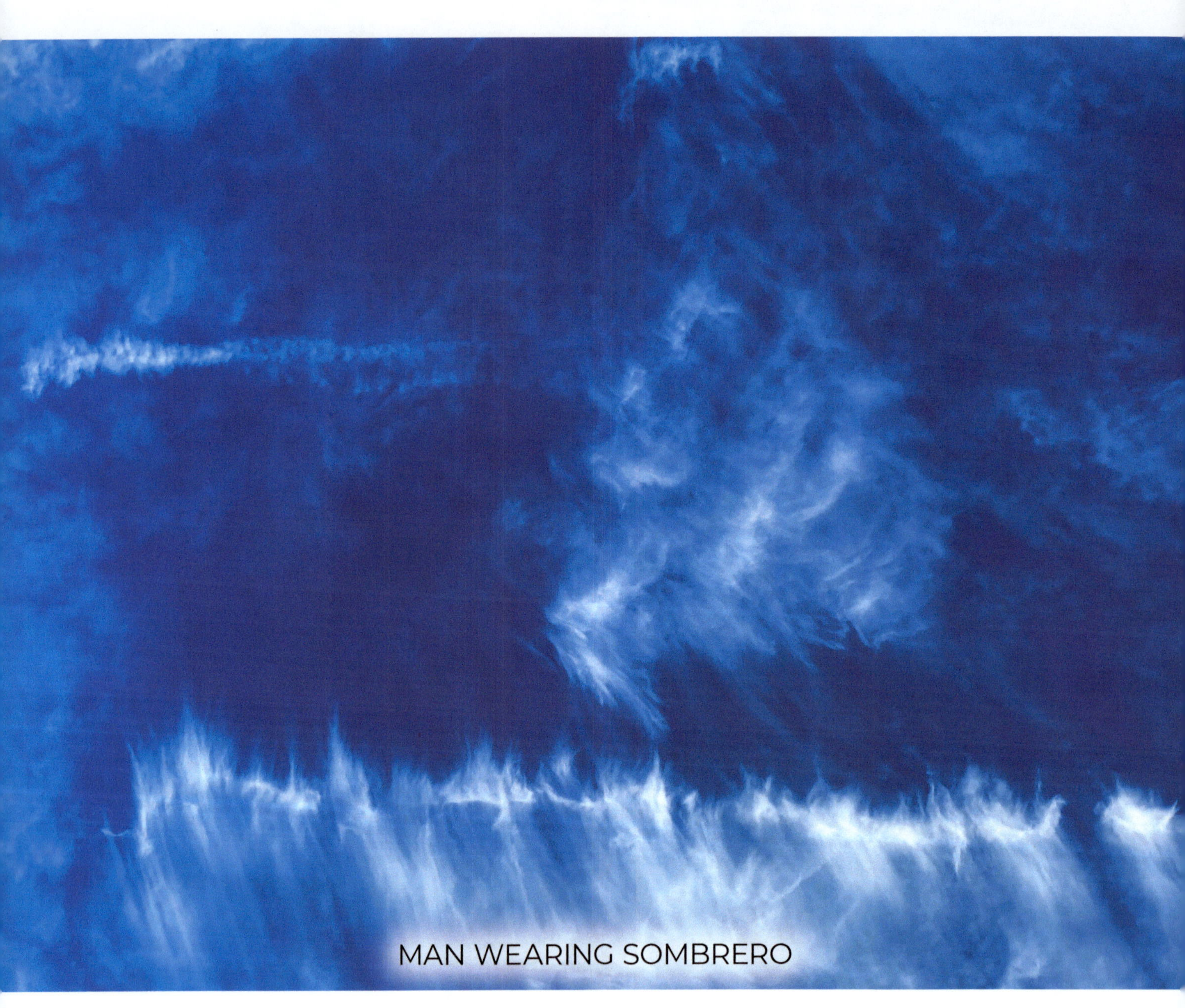

MAN WEARING SOMBRERO

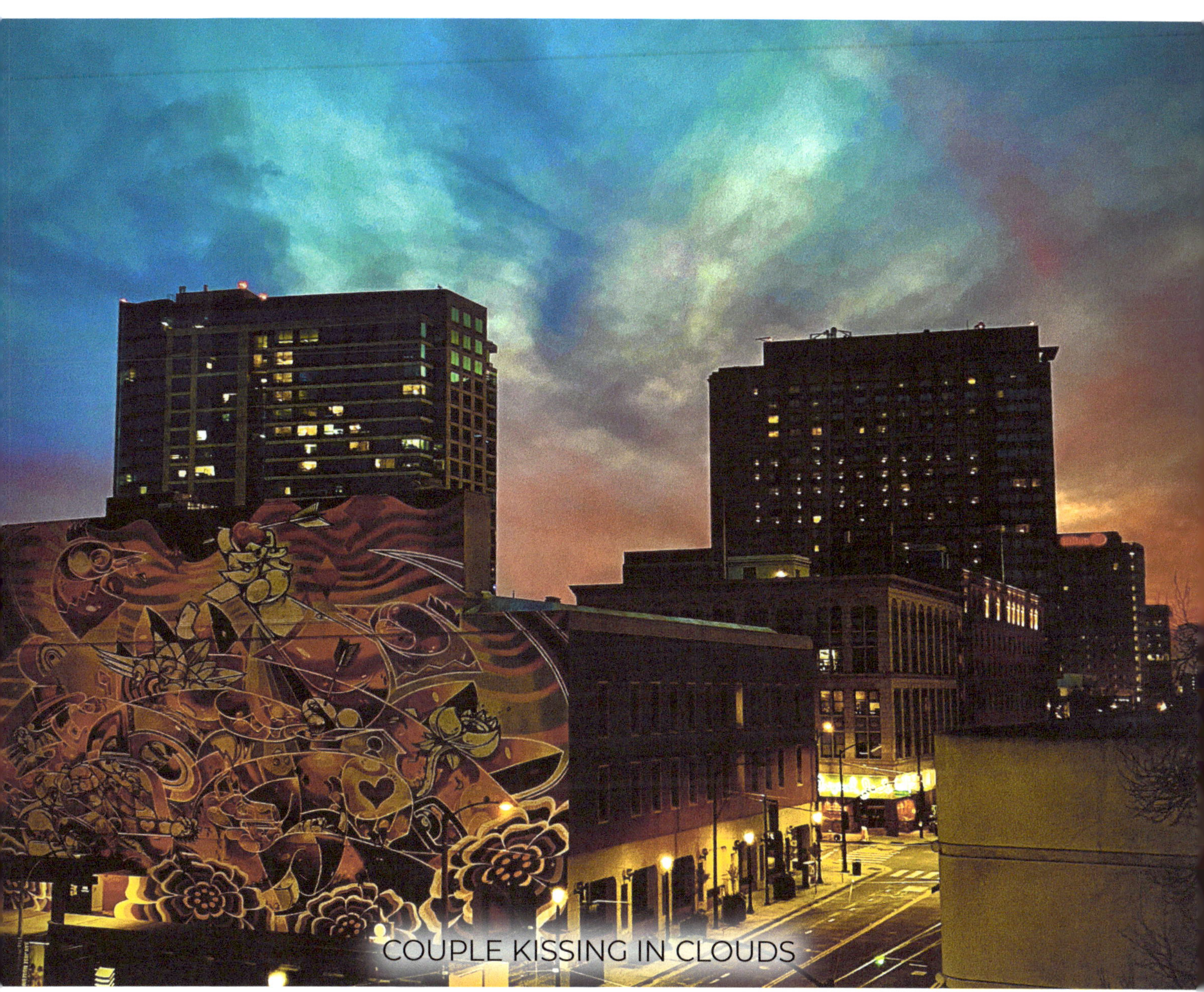
COUPLE KISSING IN CLOUDS

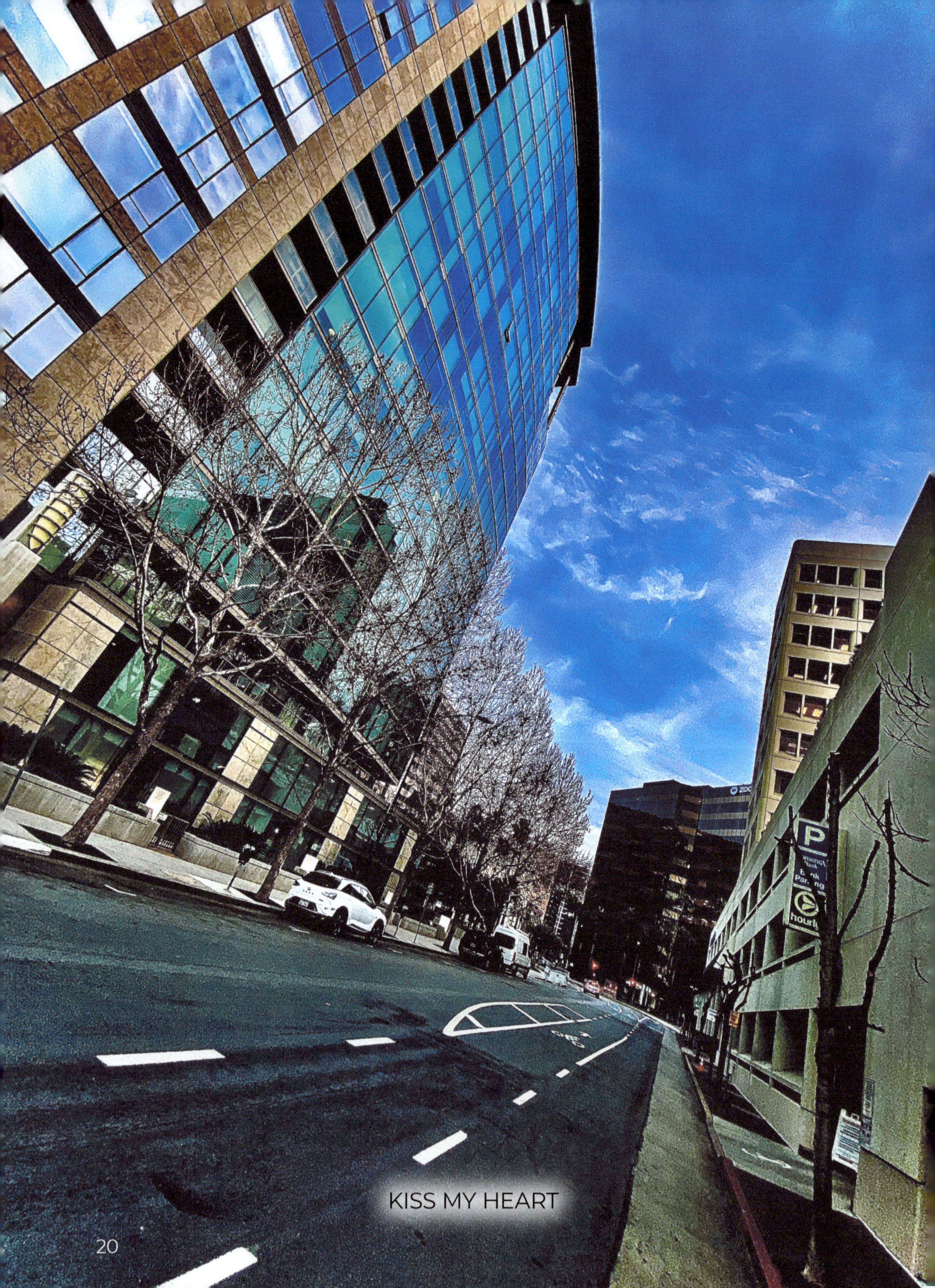

P
Parking
hourly
KISS MY HEART

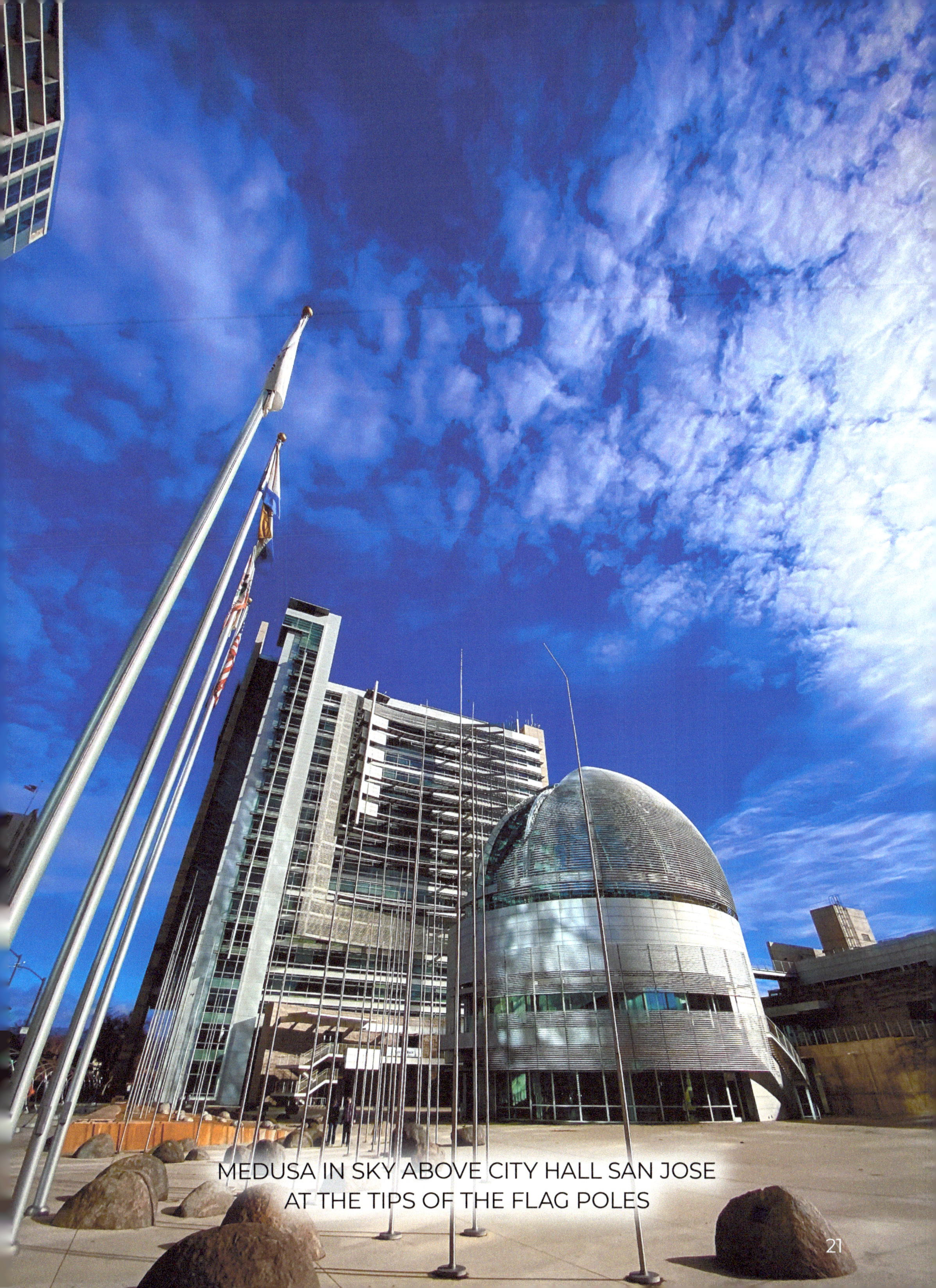

MEDUSA IN SKY ABOVE CITY HALL SAN JOSE
AT THE TIPS OF THE FLAG POLES

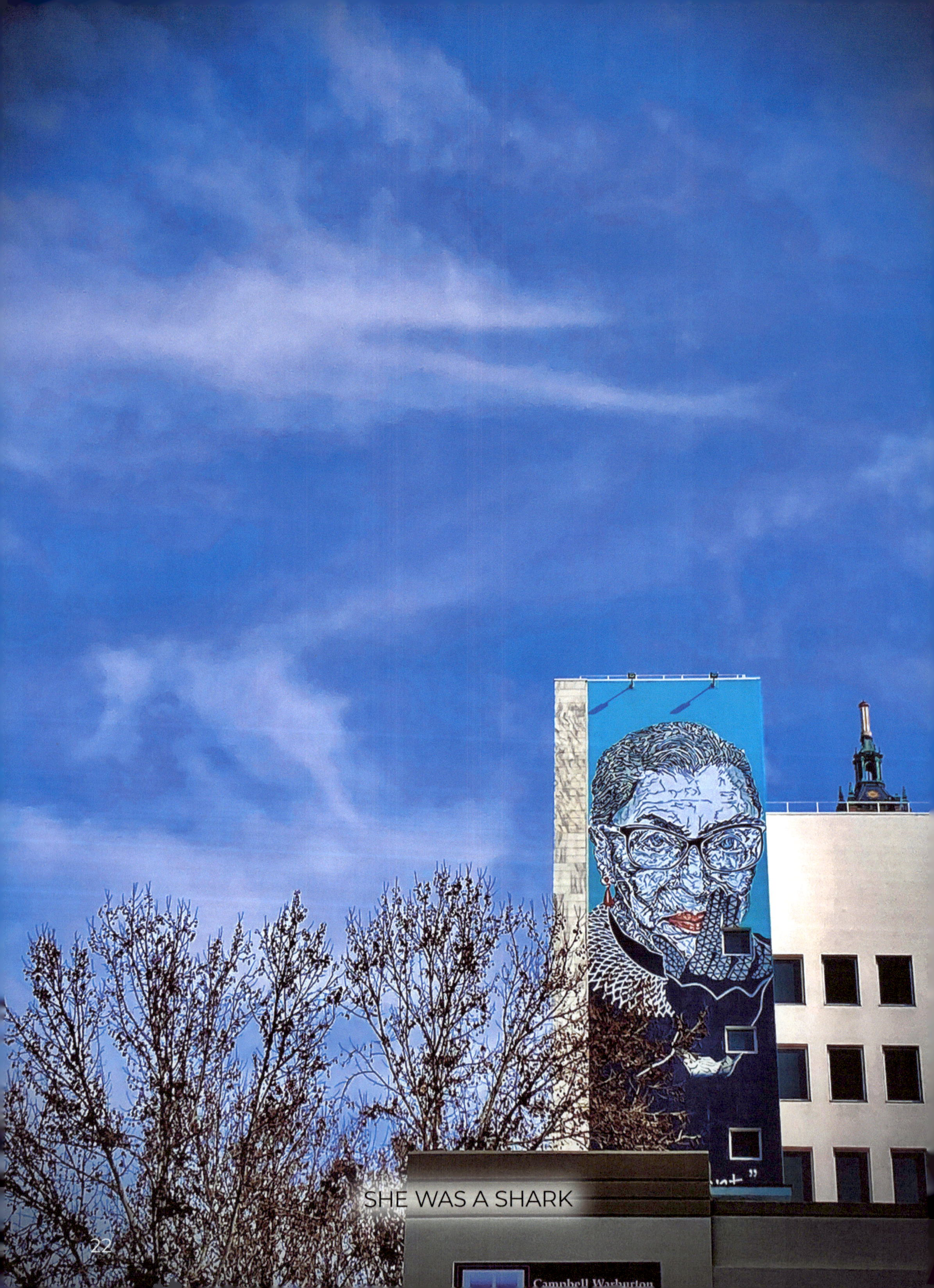

SHE WAS A SHARK

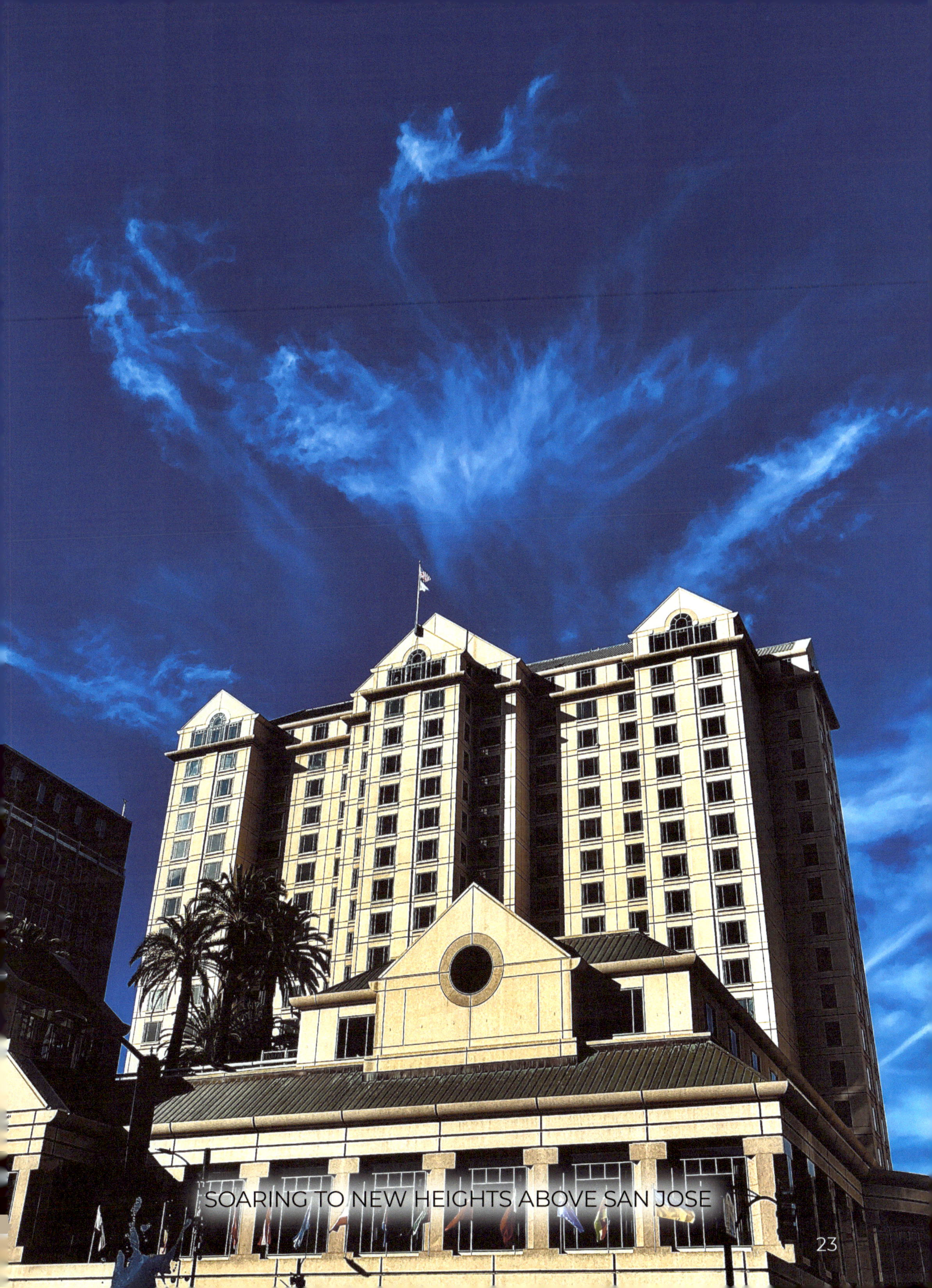

SOARING TO NEW HEIGHTS ABOVE SAN JOSE

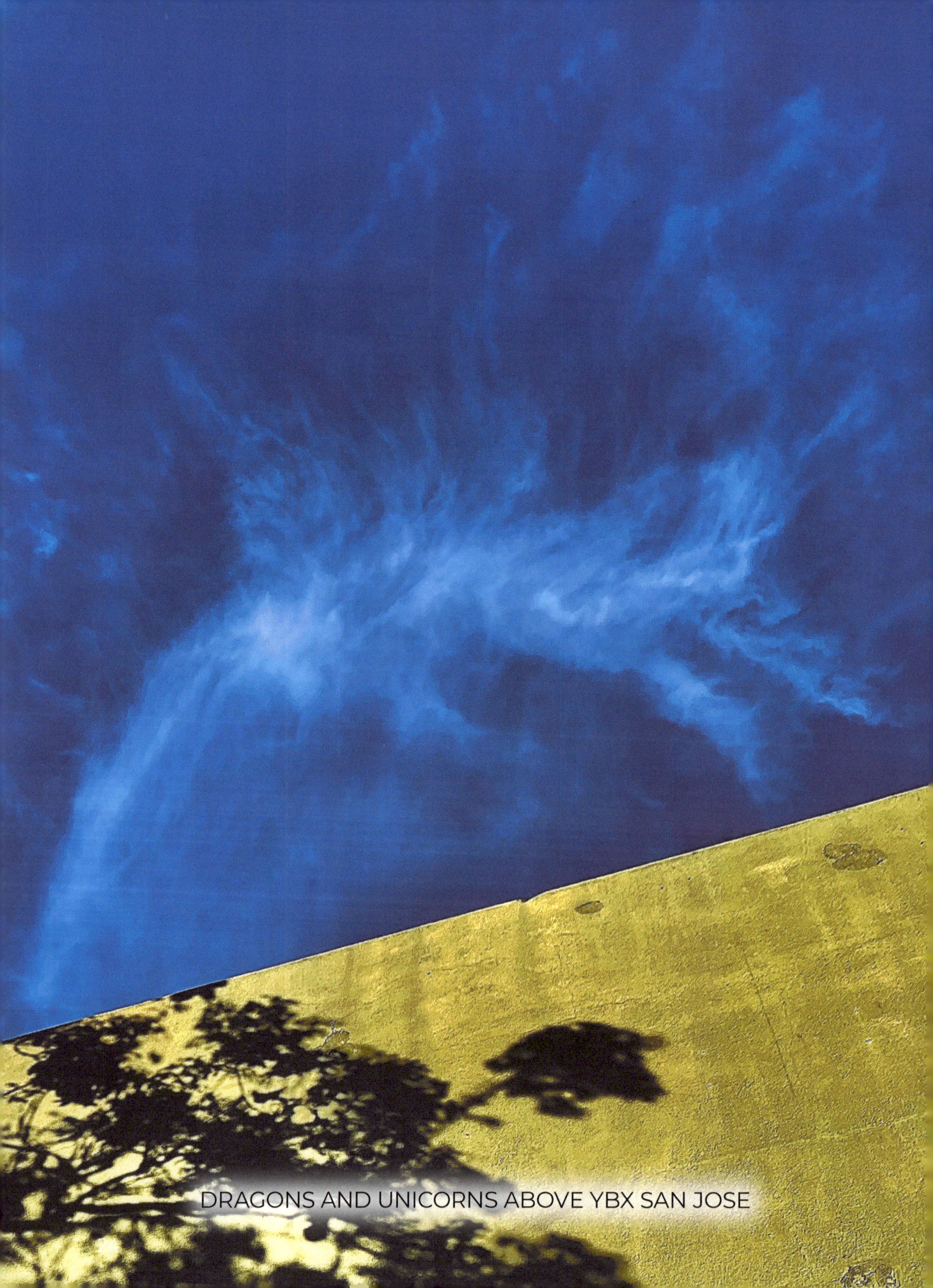

DRAGONS AND UNICORNS ABOVE YBX SAN JOSE

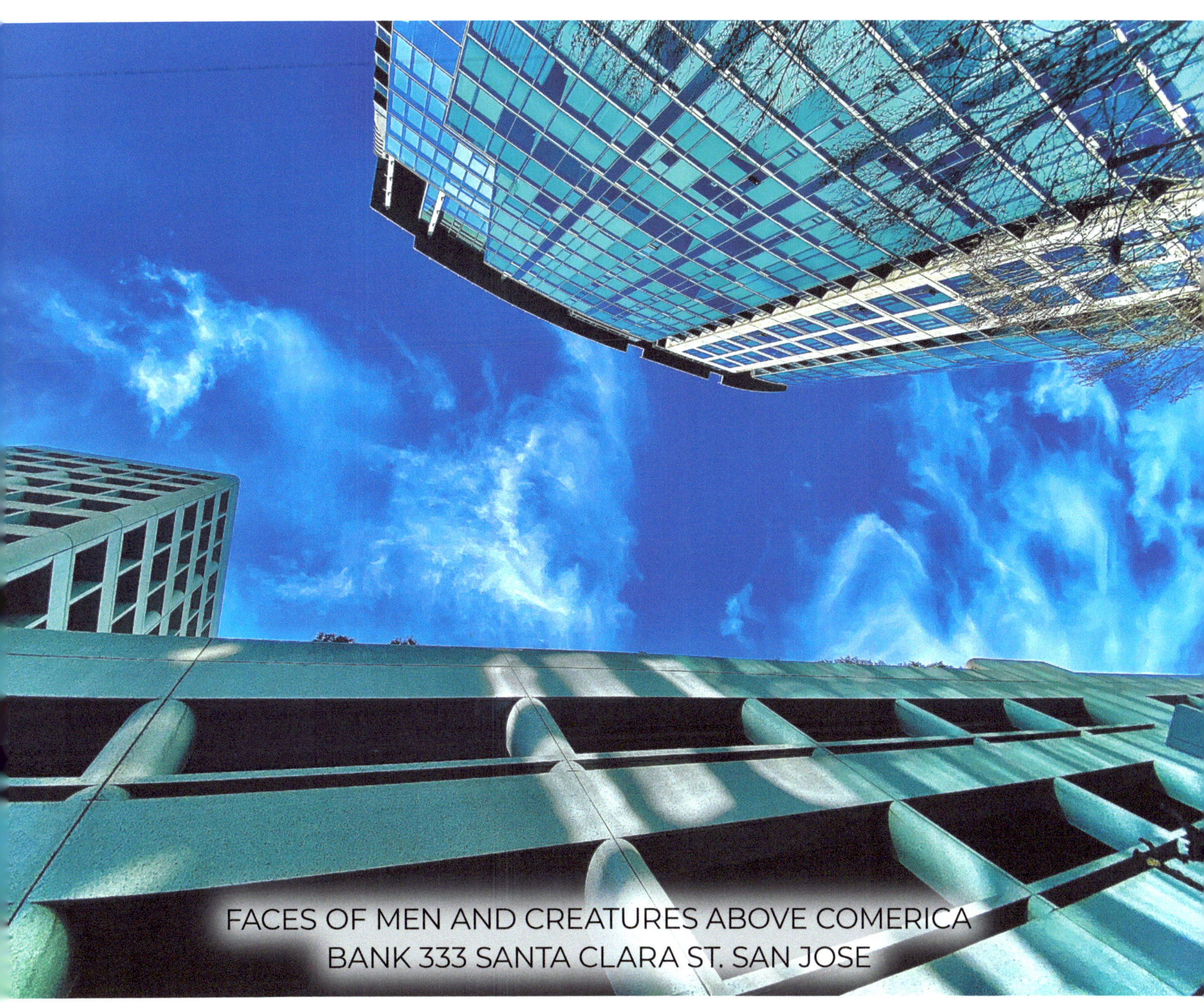

FACES OF MEN AND CREATURES ABOVE COMERICA
BANK 333 SANTA CLARA ST. SAN JOSE

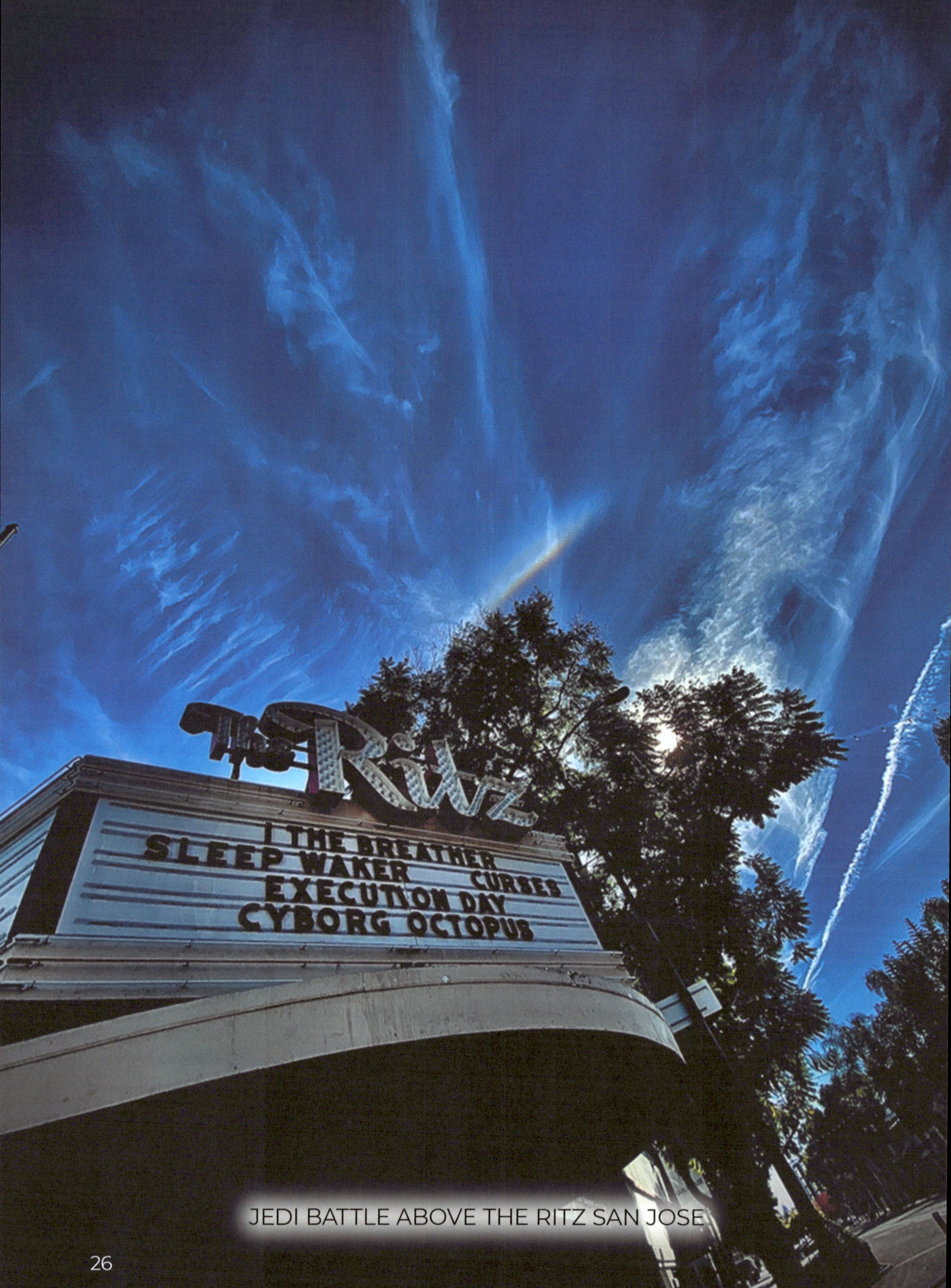

JEDI BATTLE ABOVE THE RITZ SAN JOSE

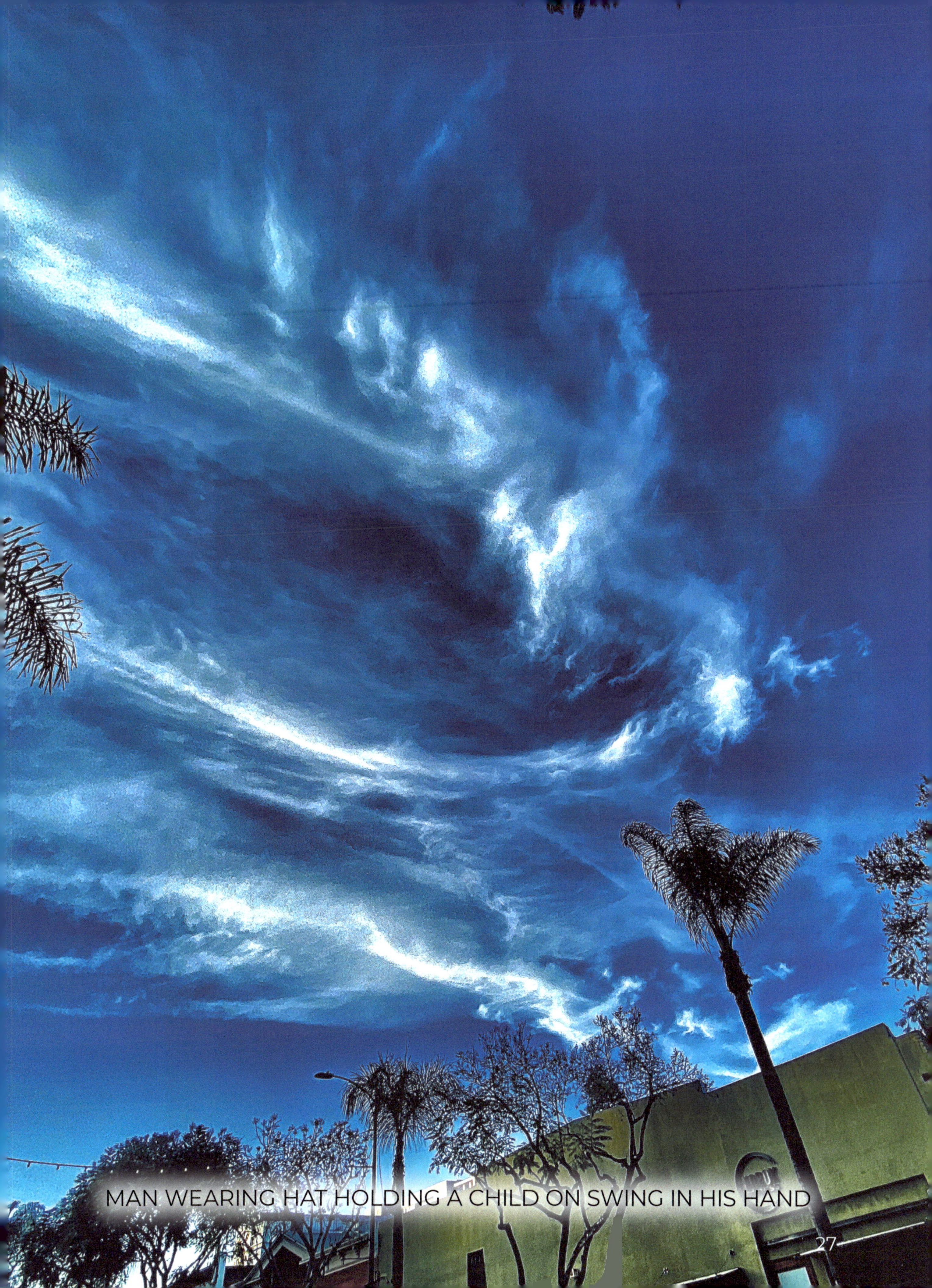

MAN WEARING HAT HOLDING A CHILD ON SWING IN HIS HAND

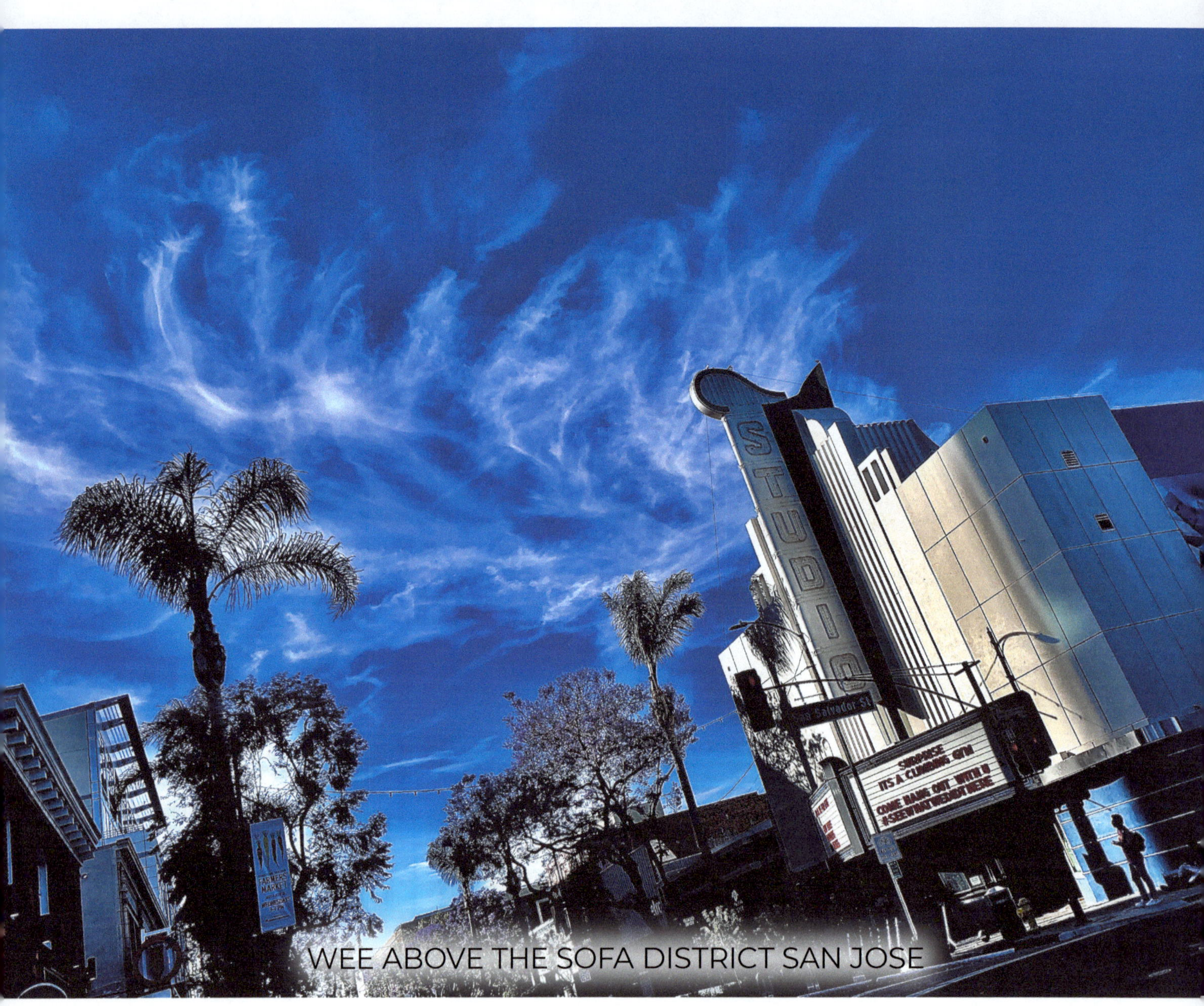
STUDIO
San Salvador St
WEE ABOVE THE SOFA DISTRICT SAN JOSE

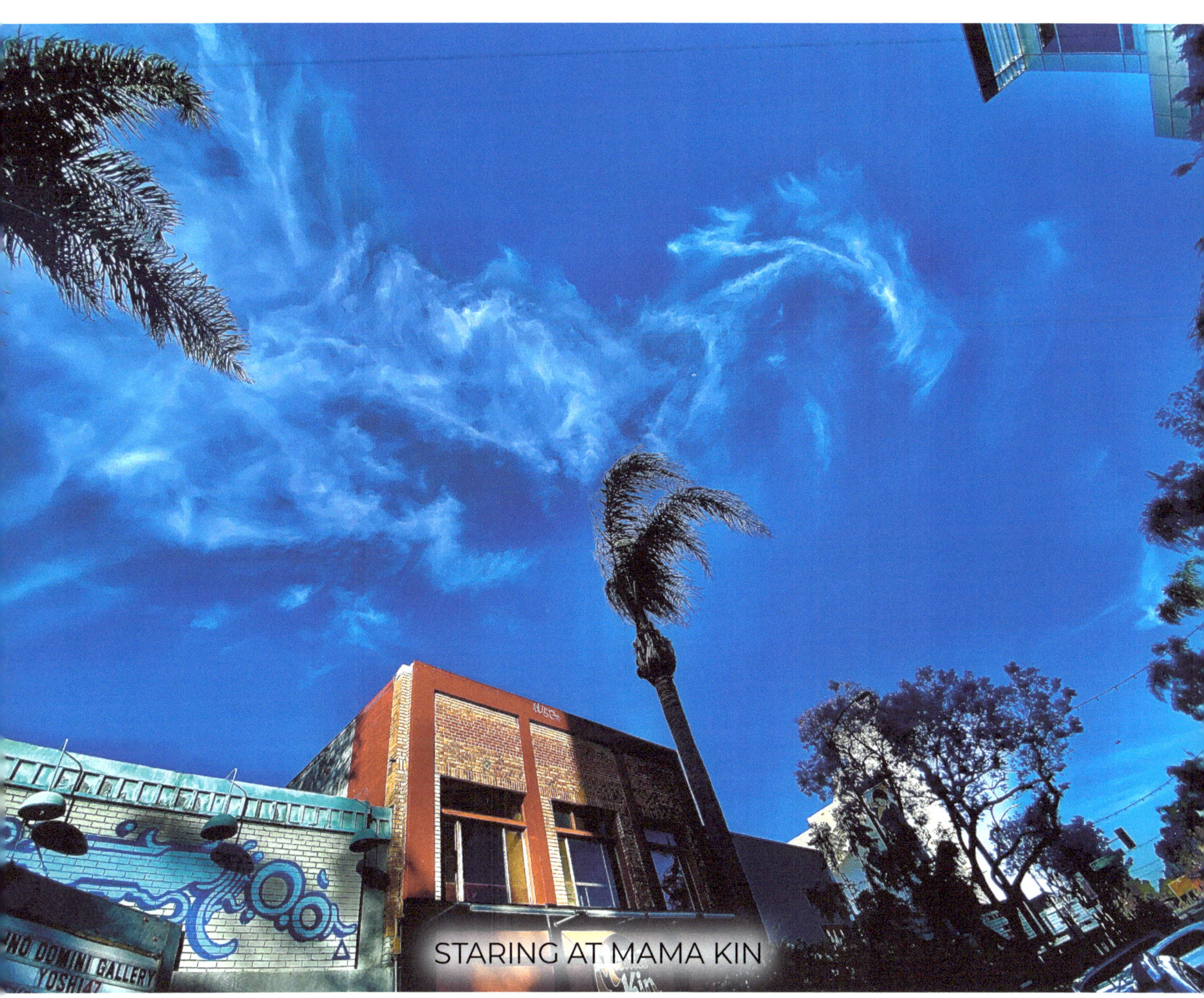
STARING AT MAMA KIN
NO DOMINI GALLERY
YOSHI'S

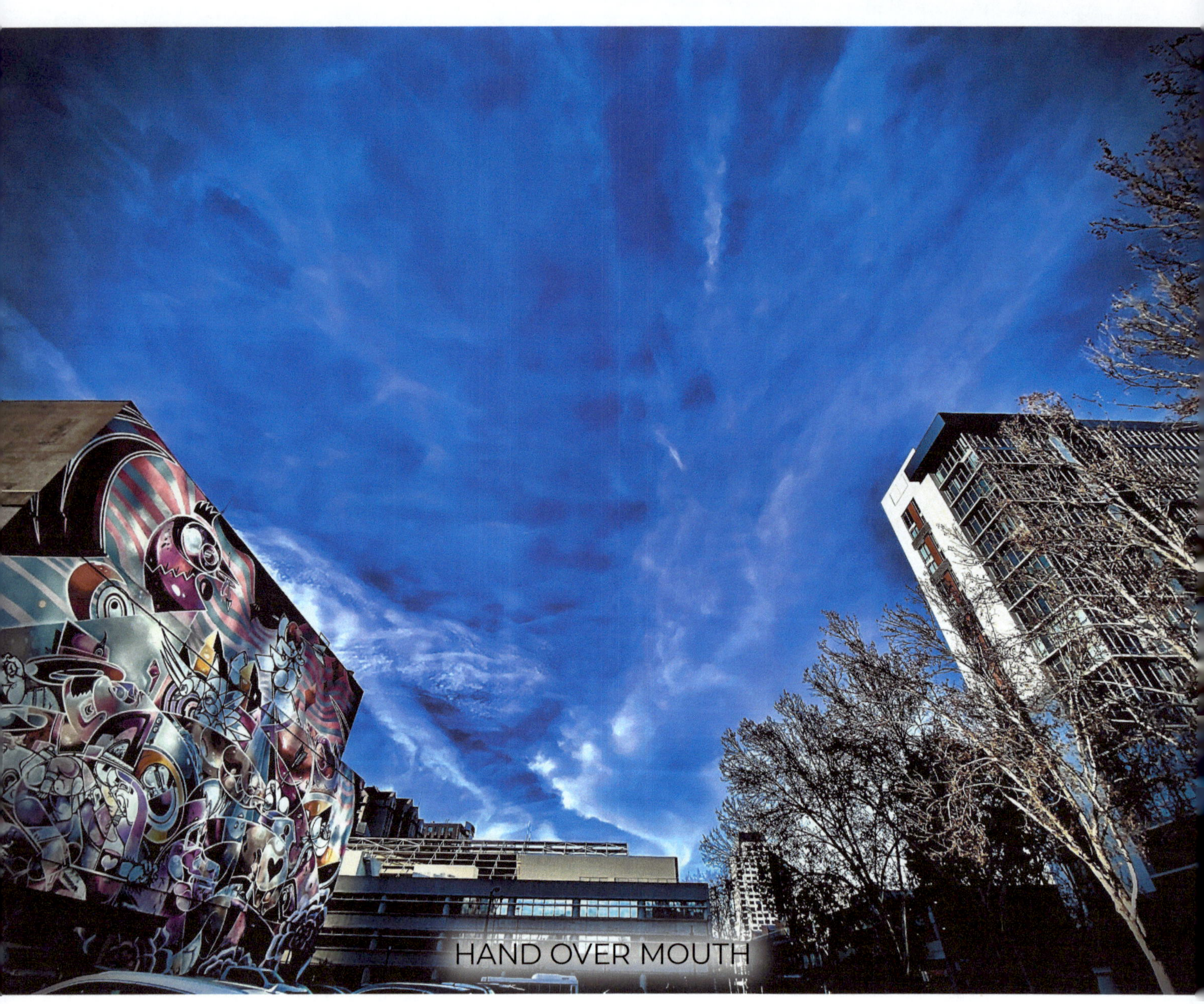
HAND OVER MOUTH

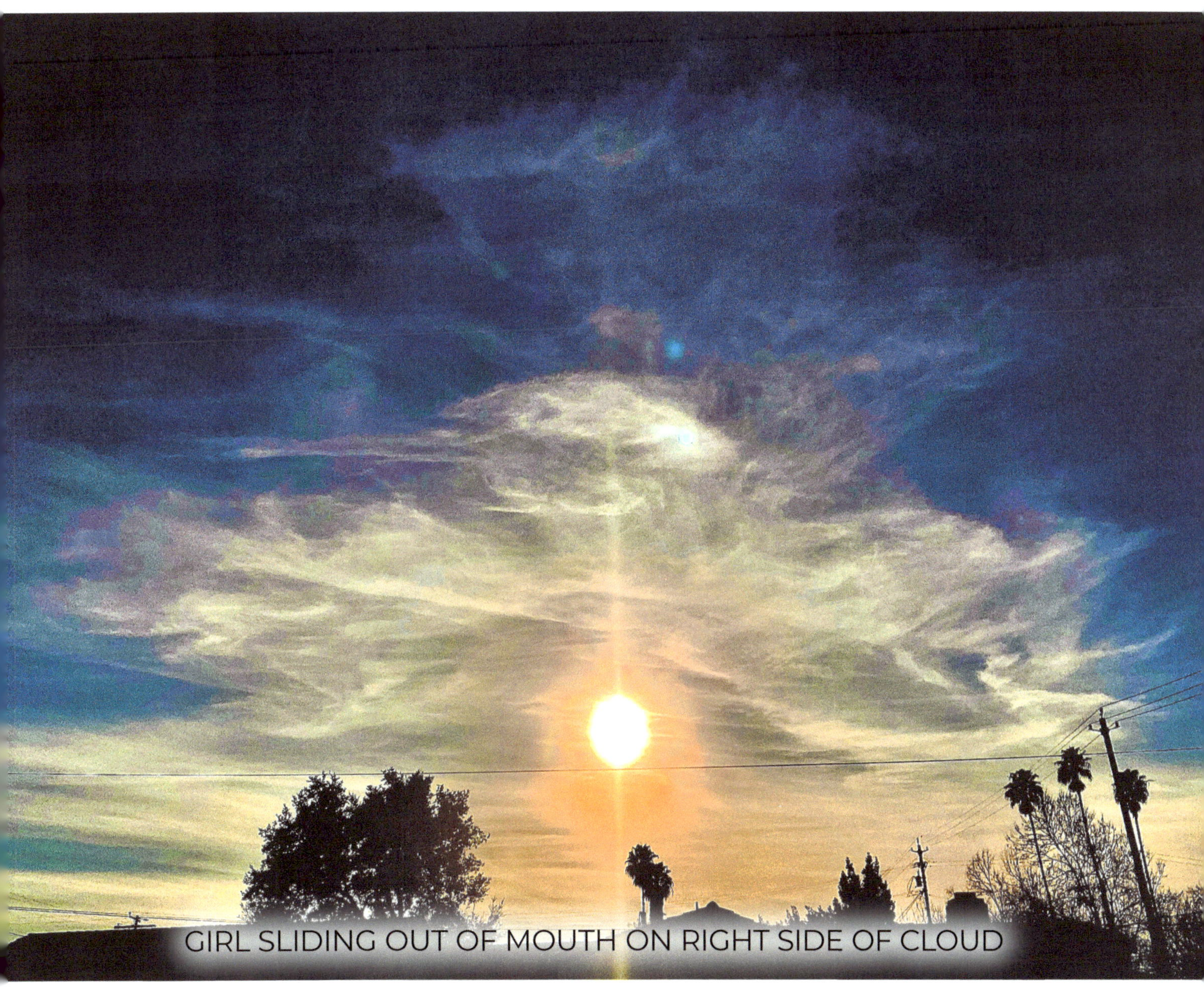

GIRL SLIDING OUT OF MOUTH ON RIGHT SIDE OF CLOUD

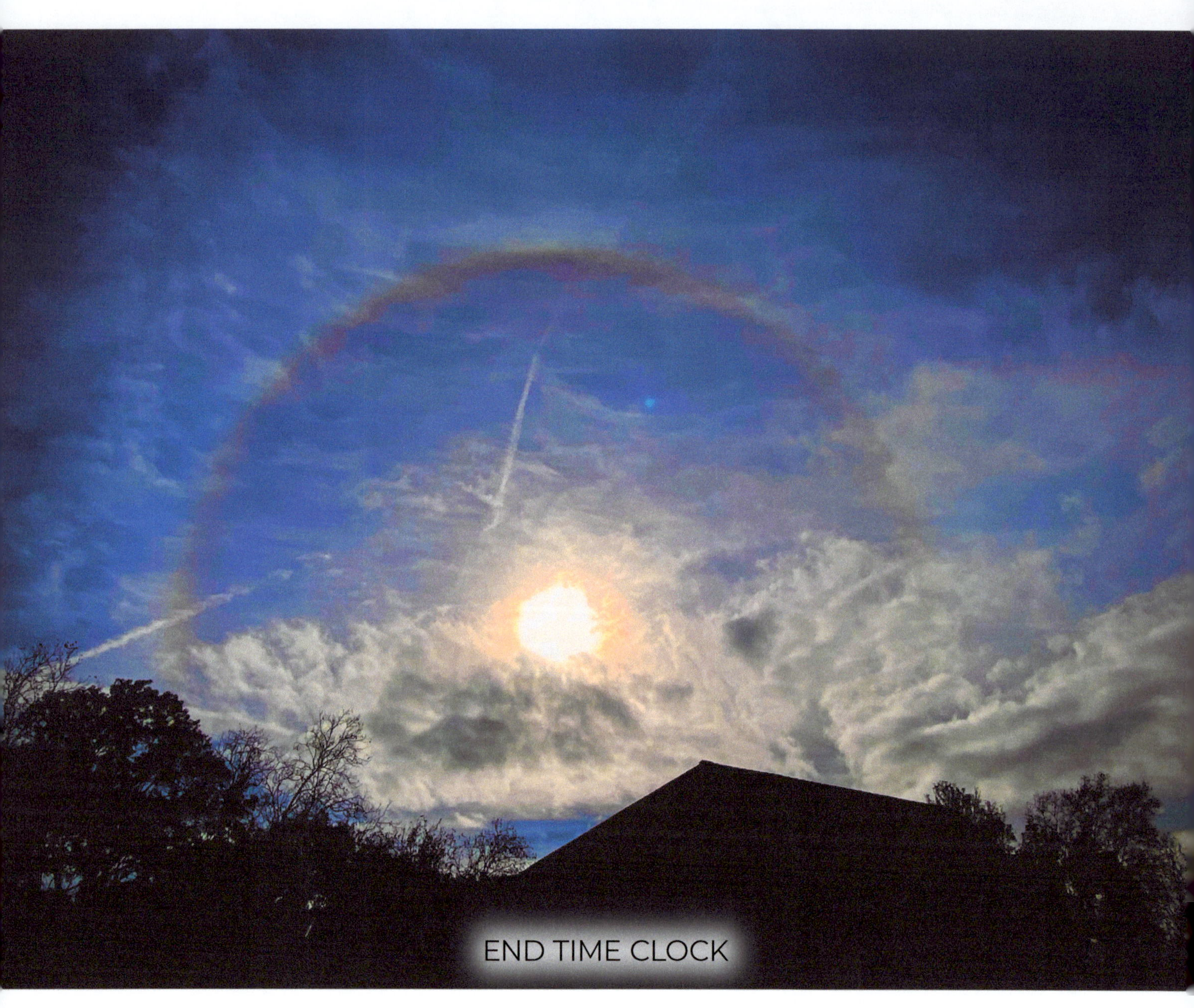

END TIME CLOCK

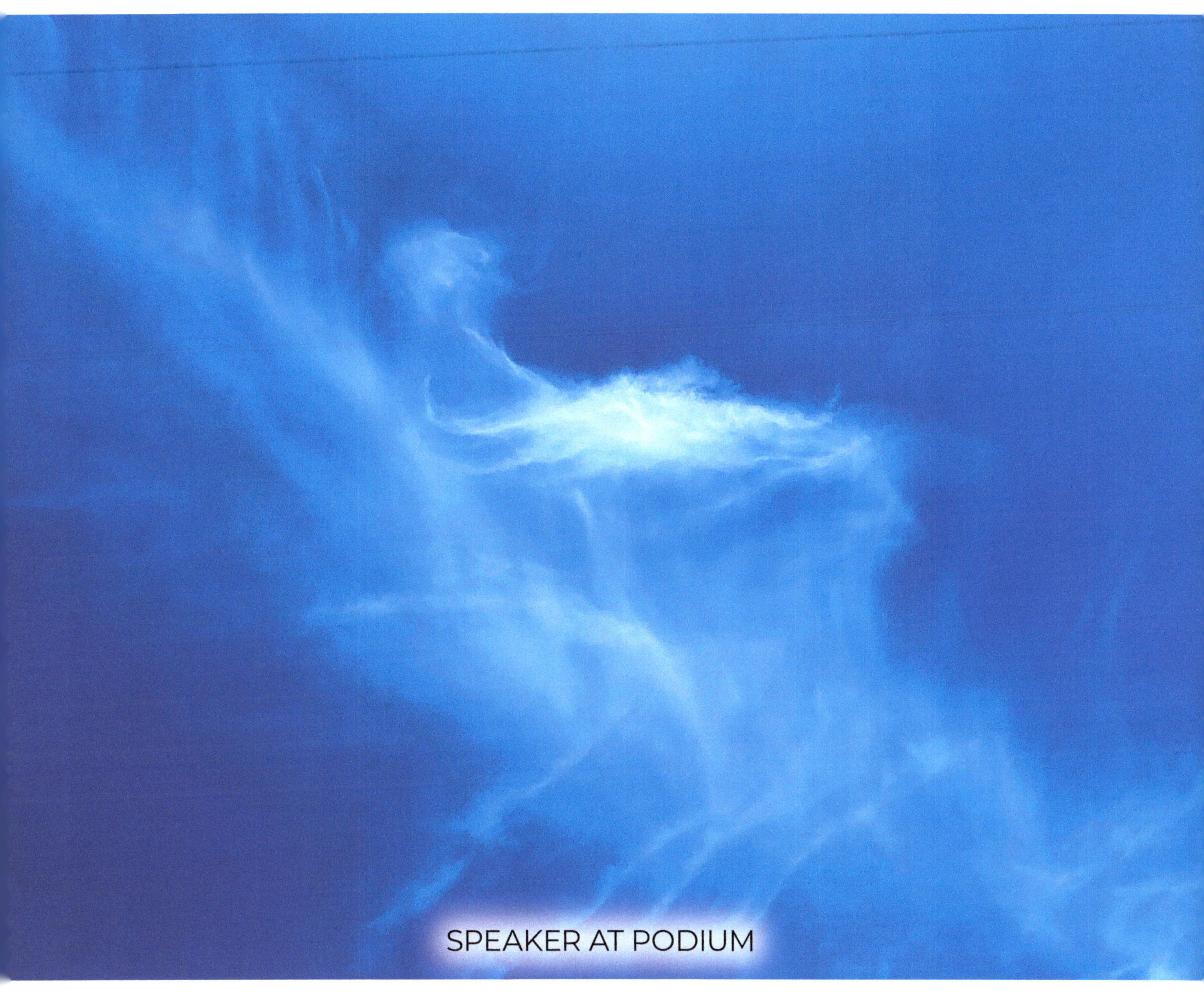

SPEAKER AT PODIUM

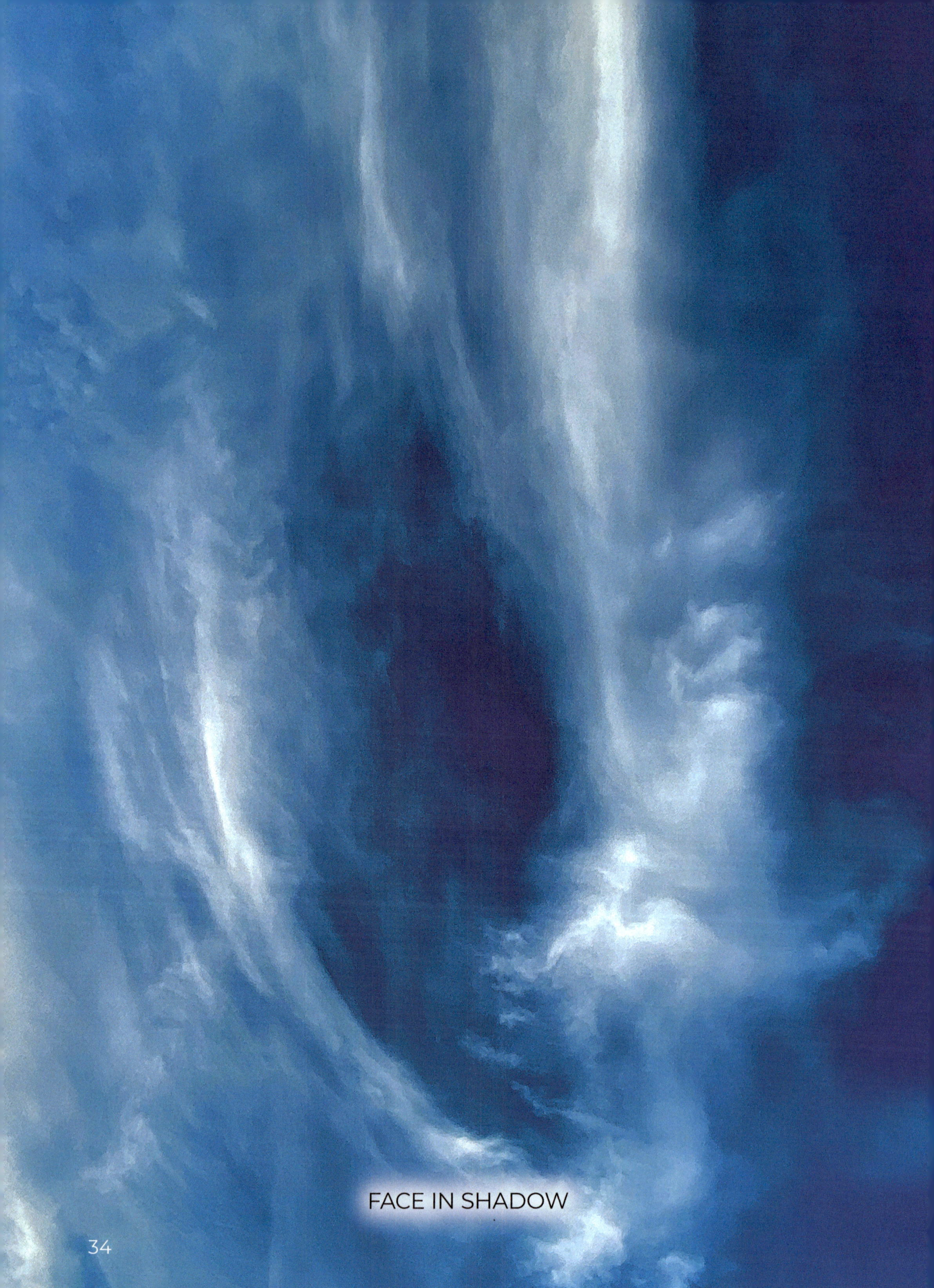

FACE IN SHADOW

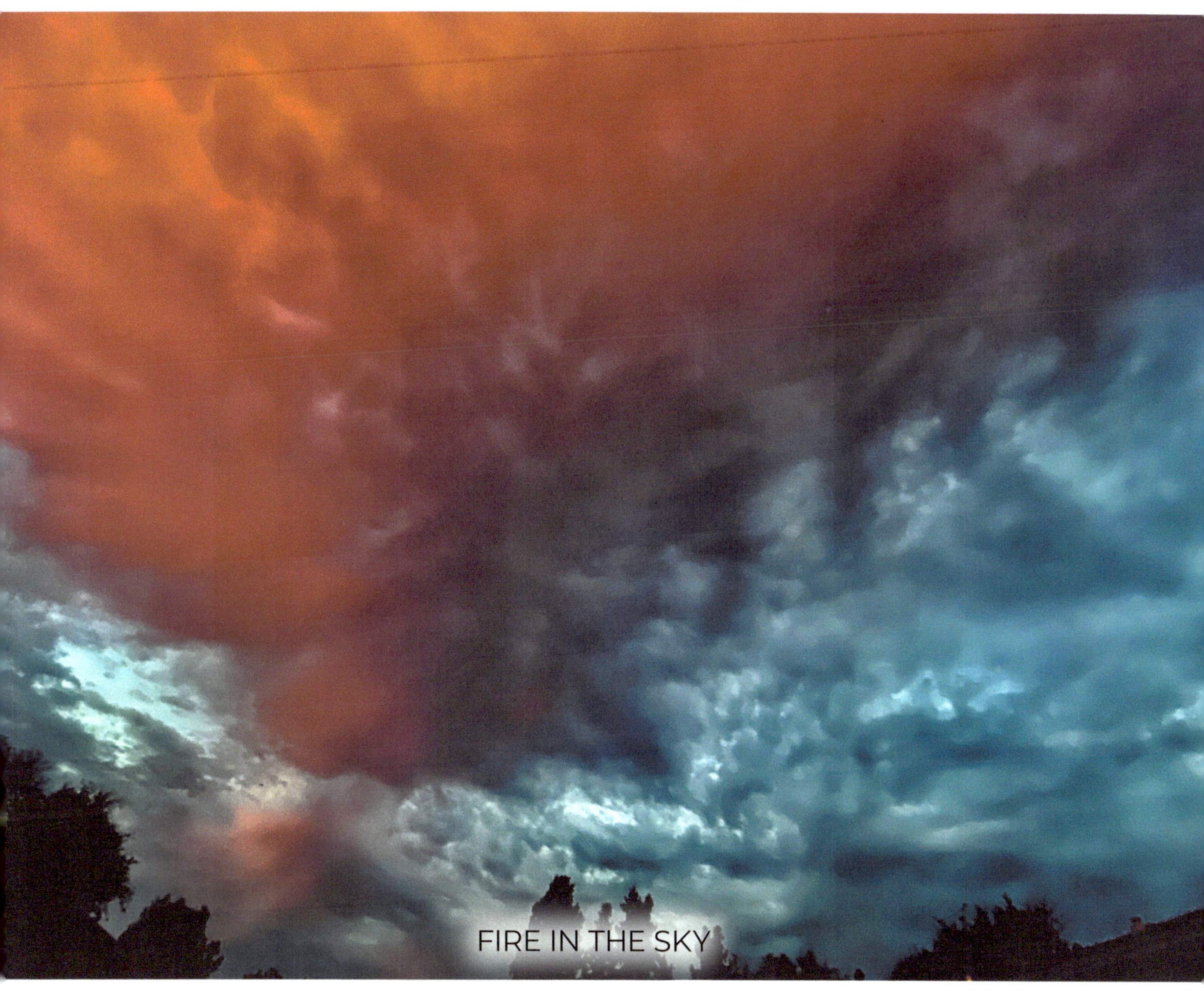
FIRE IN THE SKY

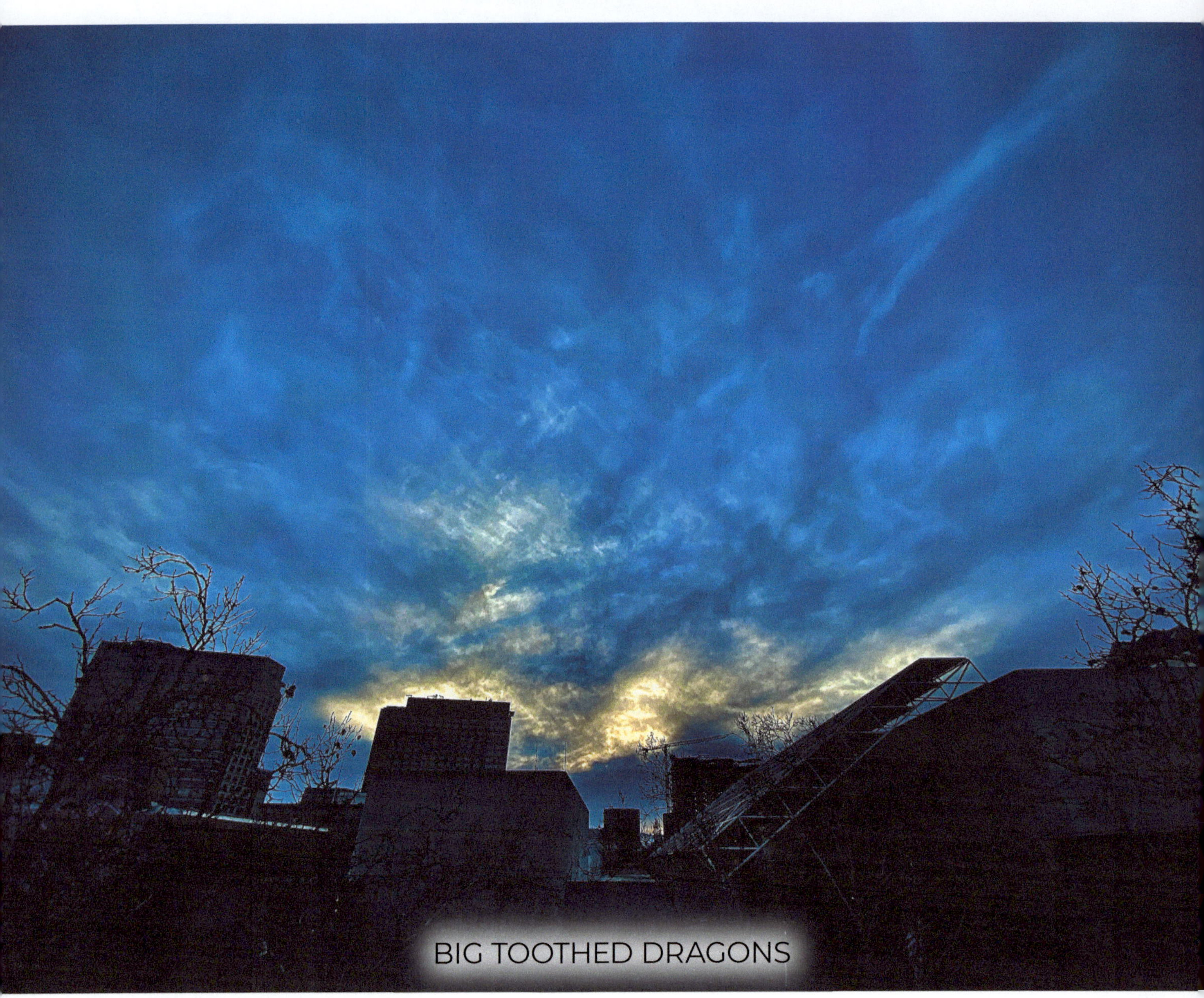

BIG TOOTHED DRAGONS

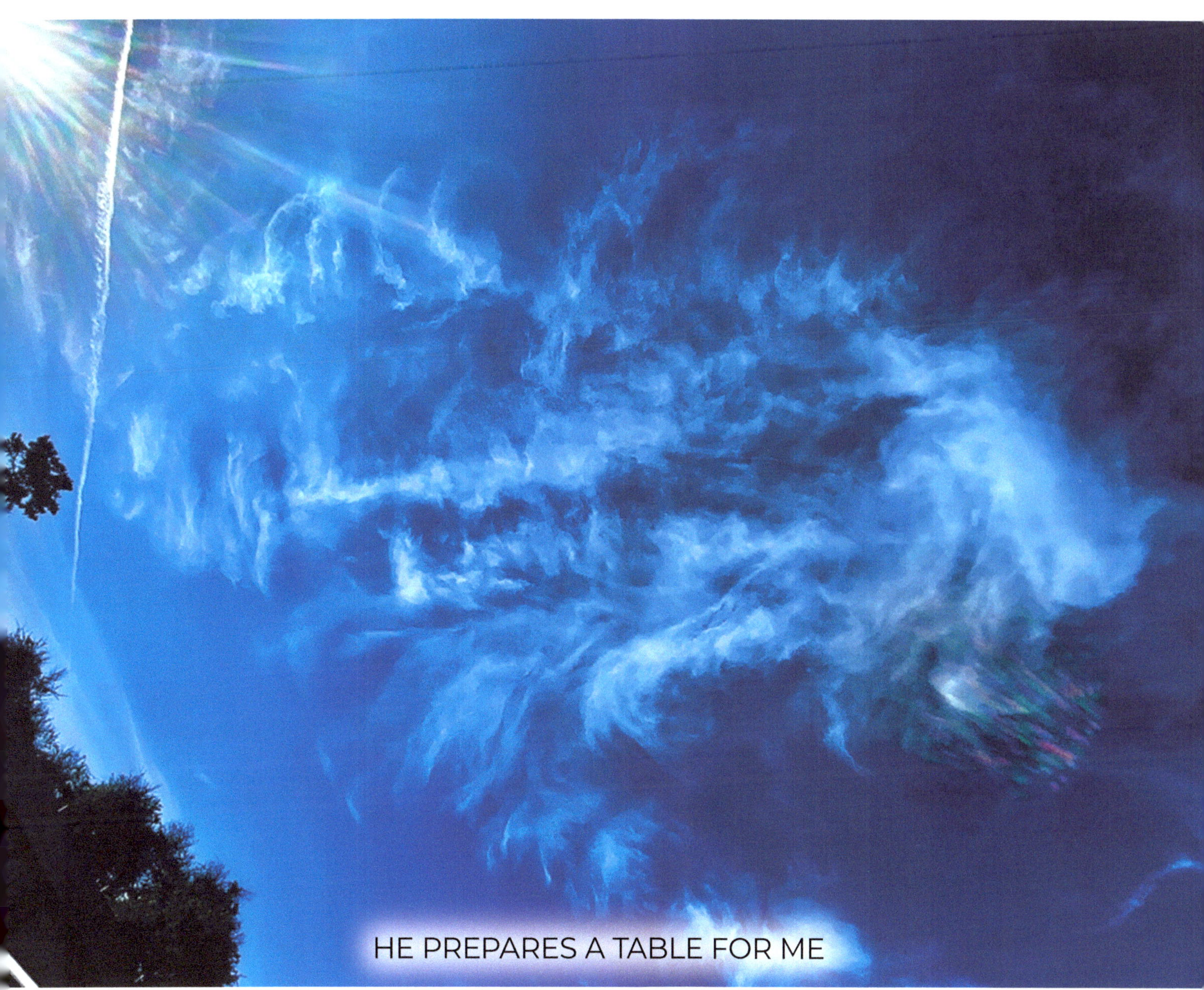

HE PREPARES A TABLE FOR ME

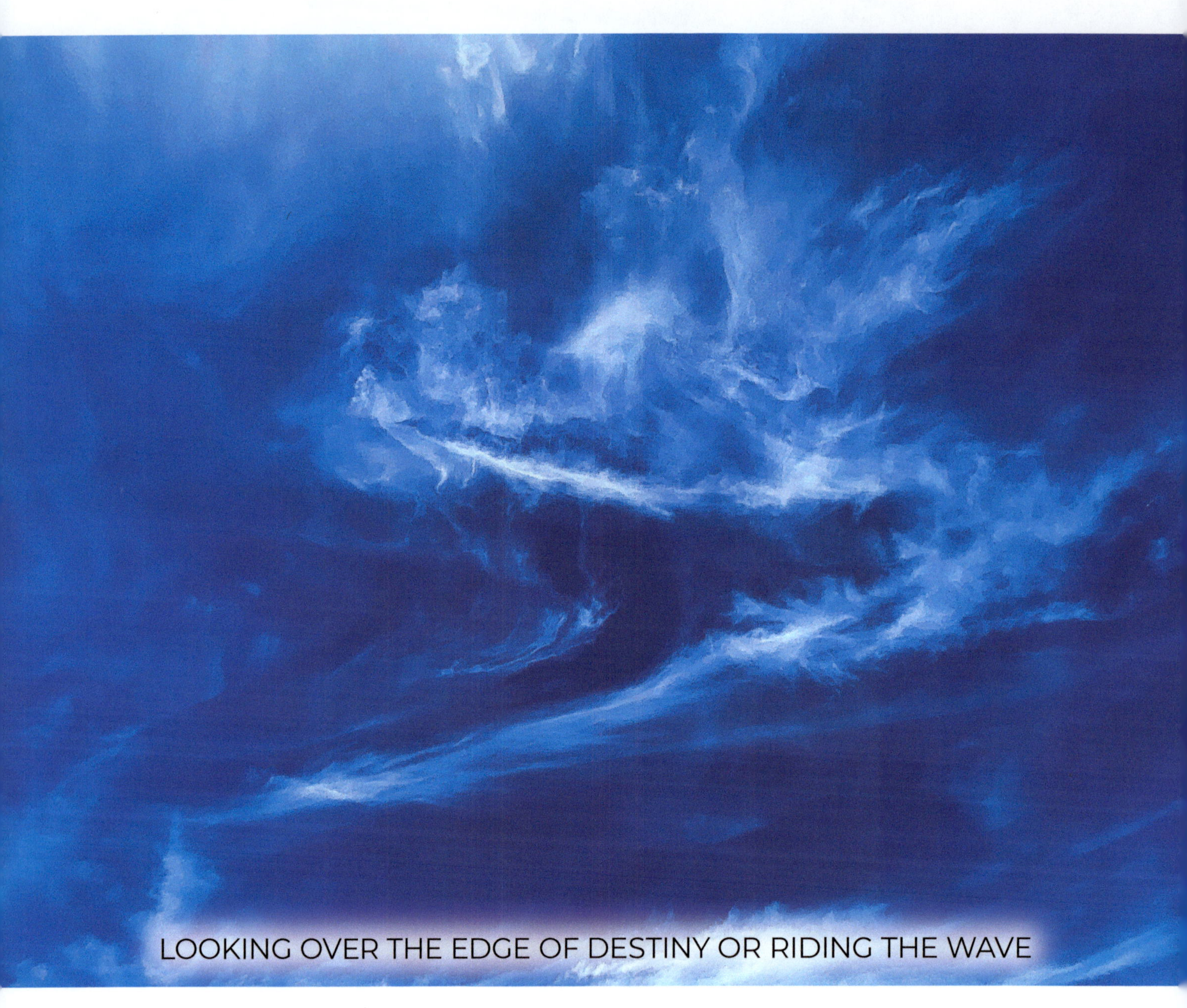

LOOKING OVER THE EDGE OF DESTINY OR RIDING THE WAVE

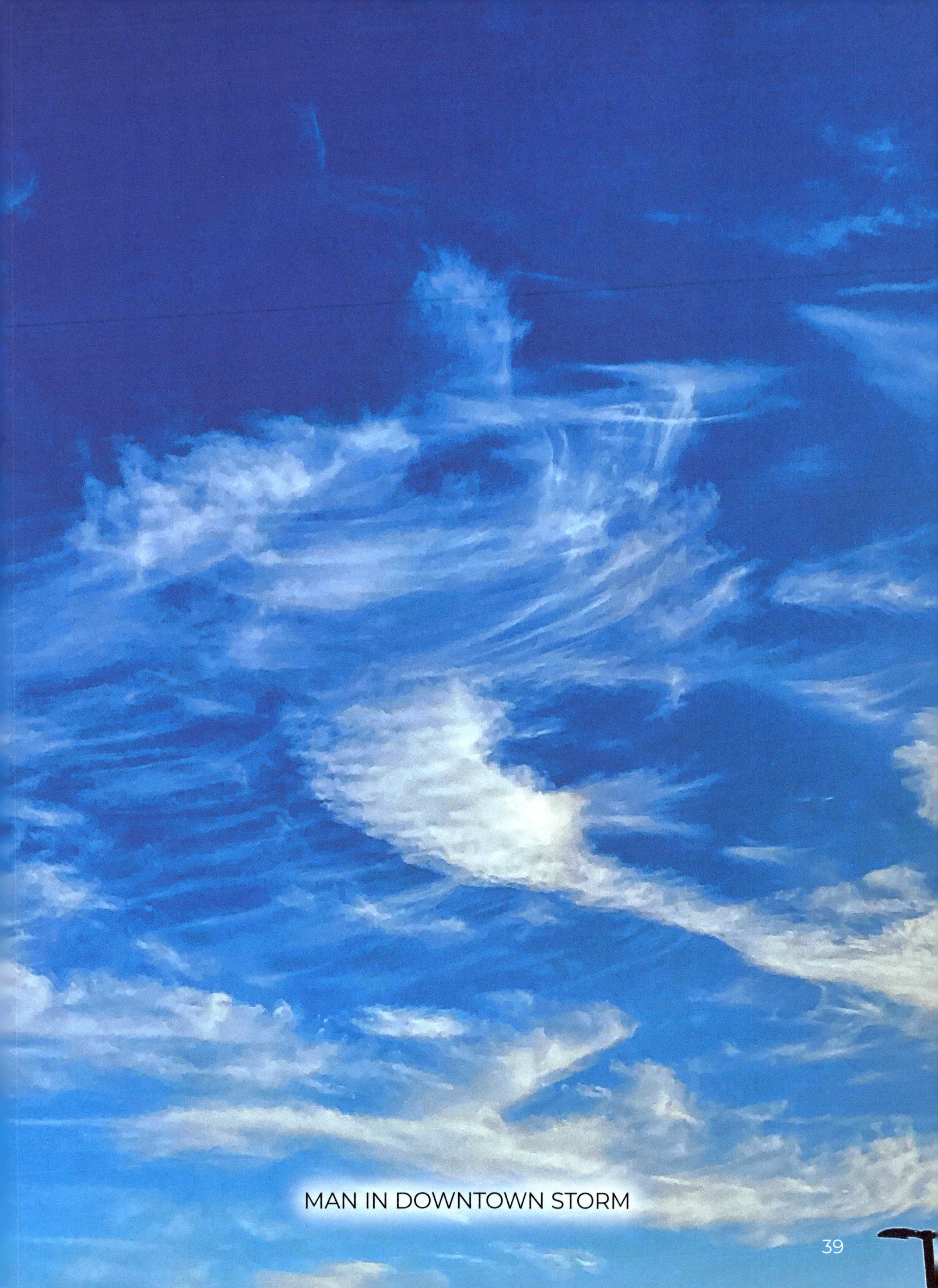

MAN IN DOWNTOWN STORM

WARRIOR WITH LITE SABER

TINKERBELL

SHINING STAR PRINCESS

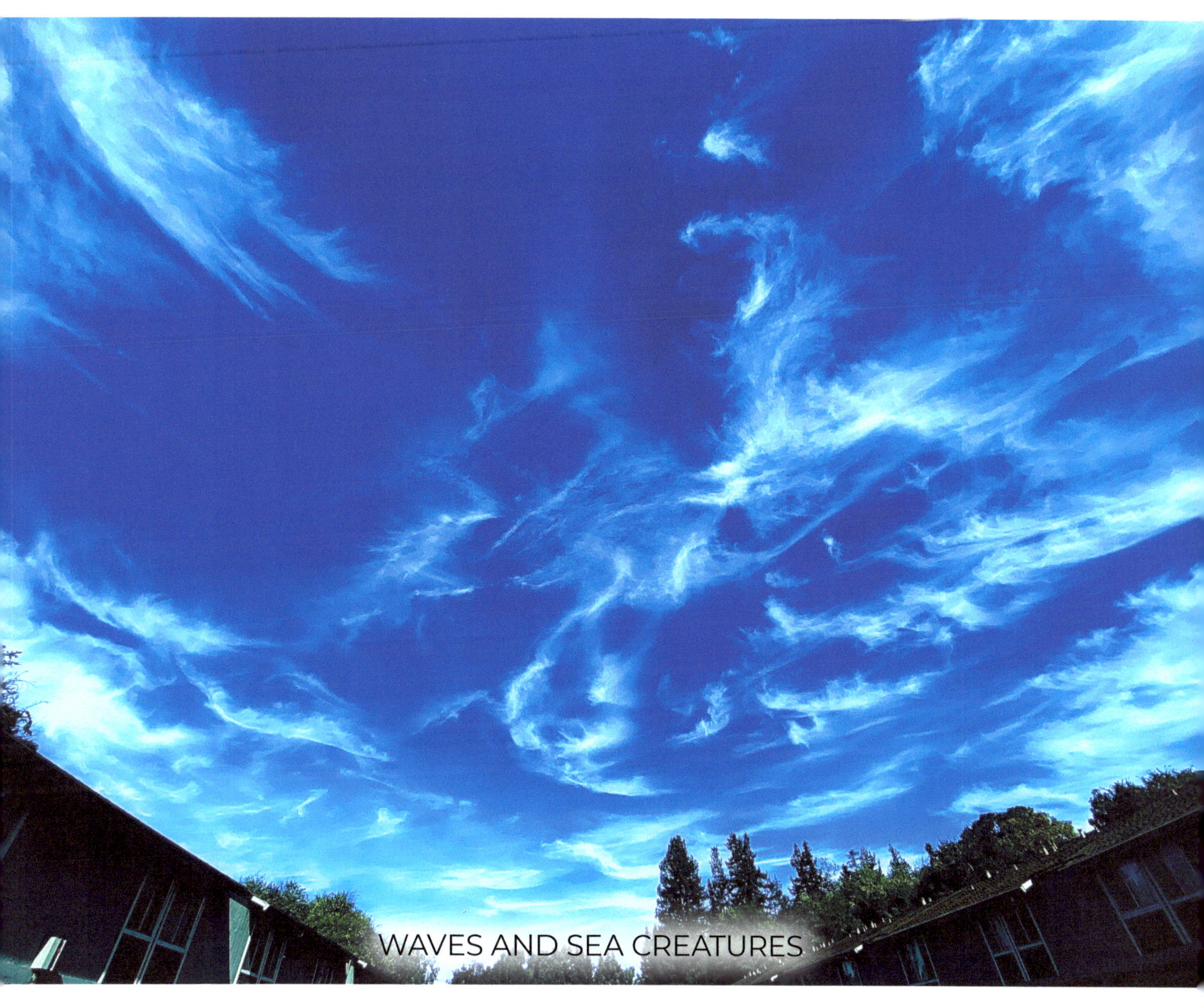
WAVES AND SEA CREATURES

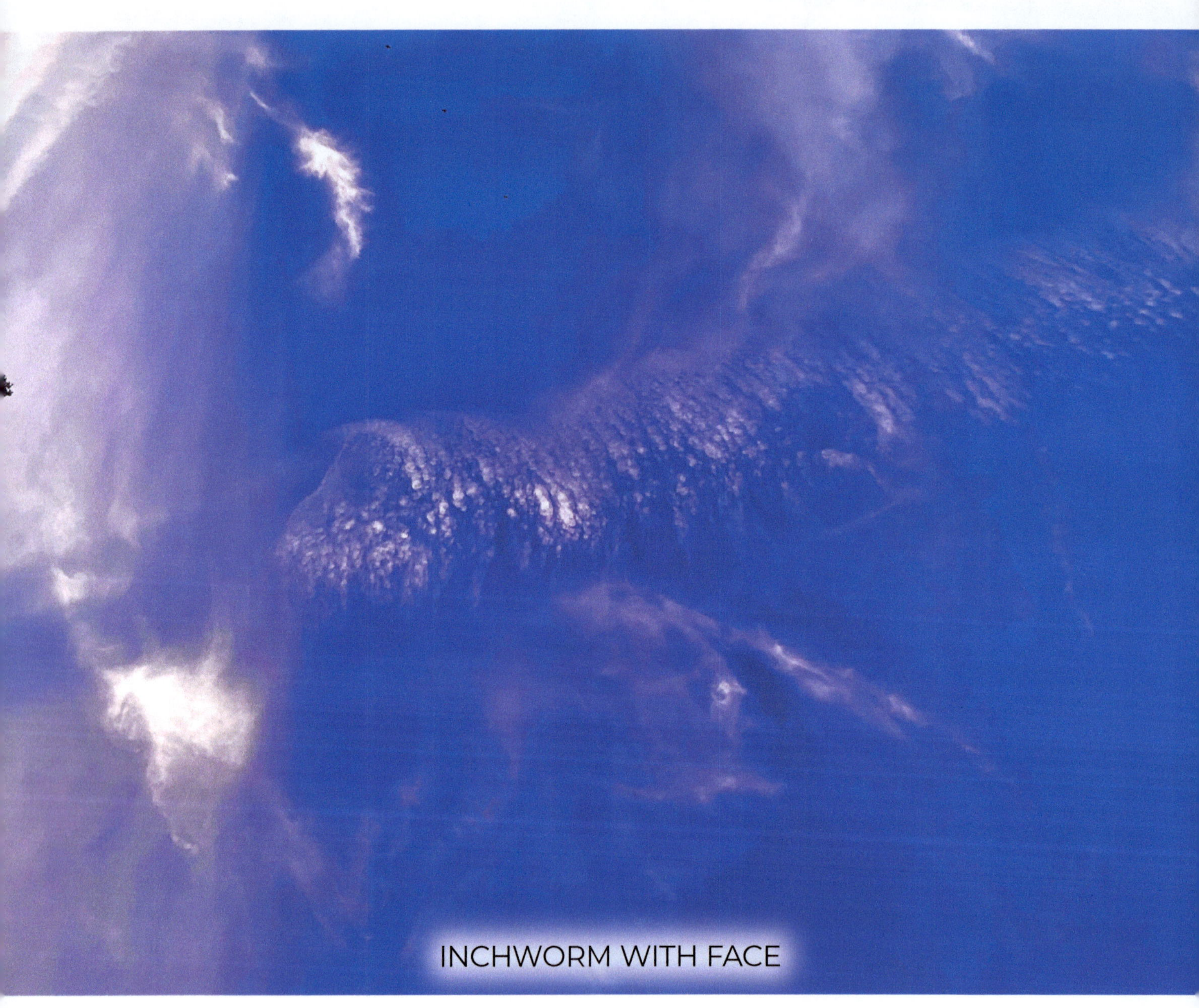

INCHWORM WITH FACE

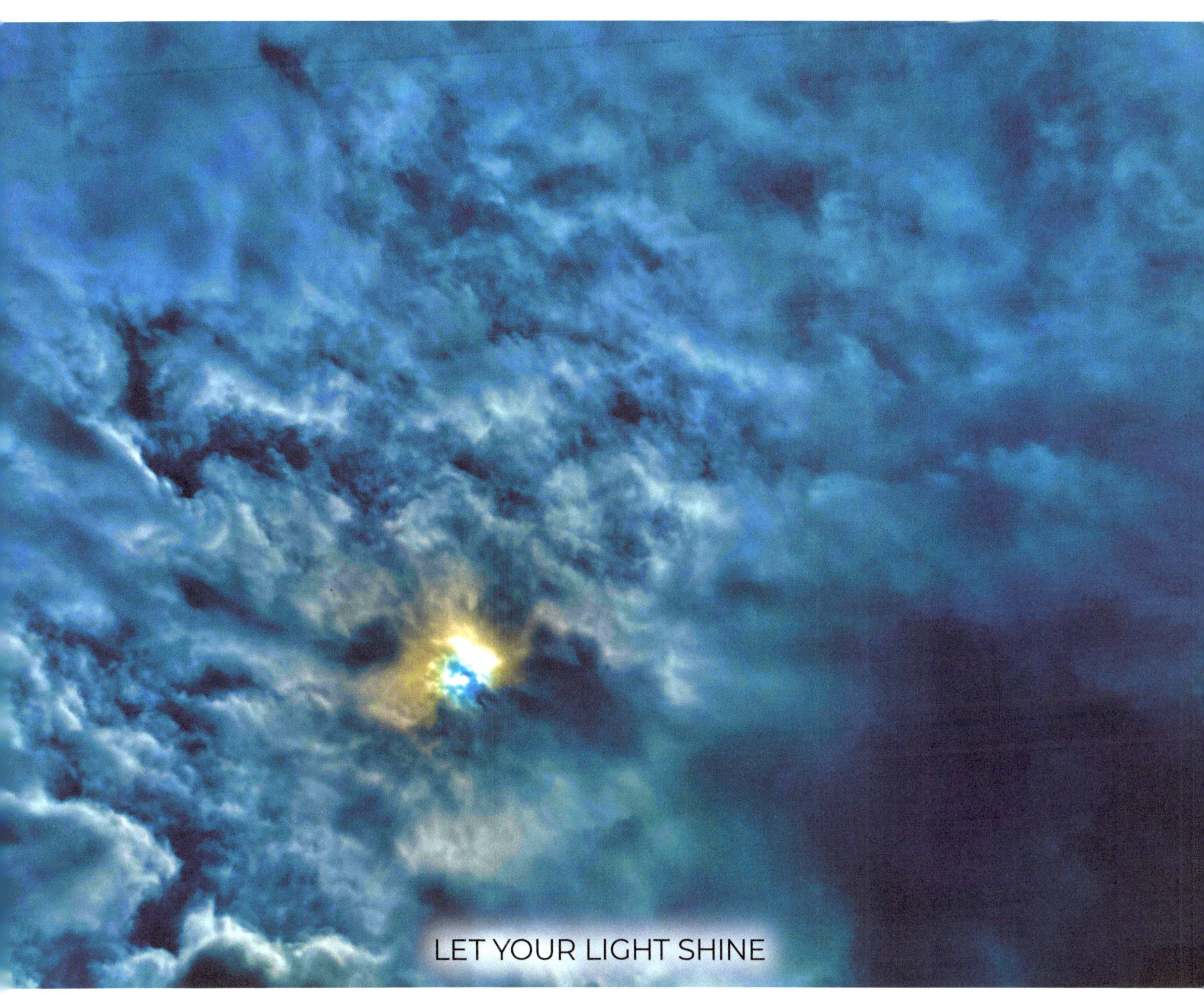
LET YOUR LIGHT SHINE

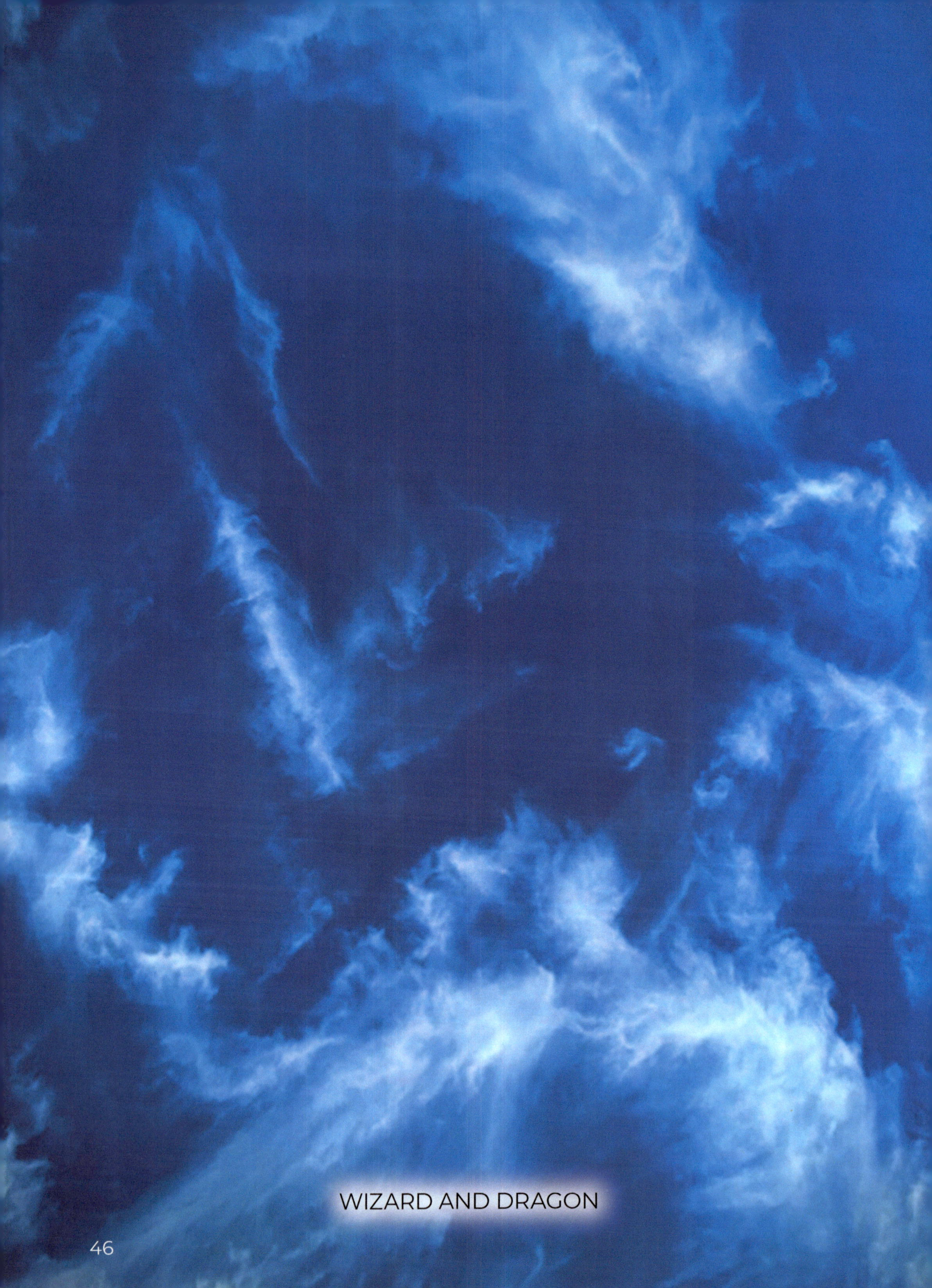

WIZARD AND DRAGON

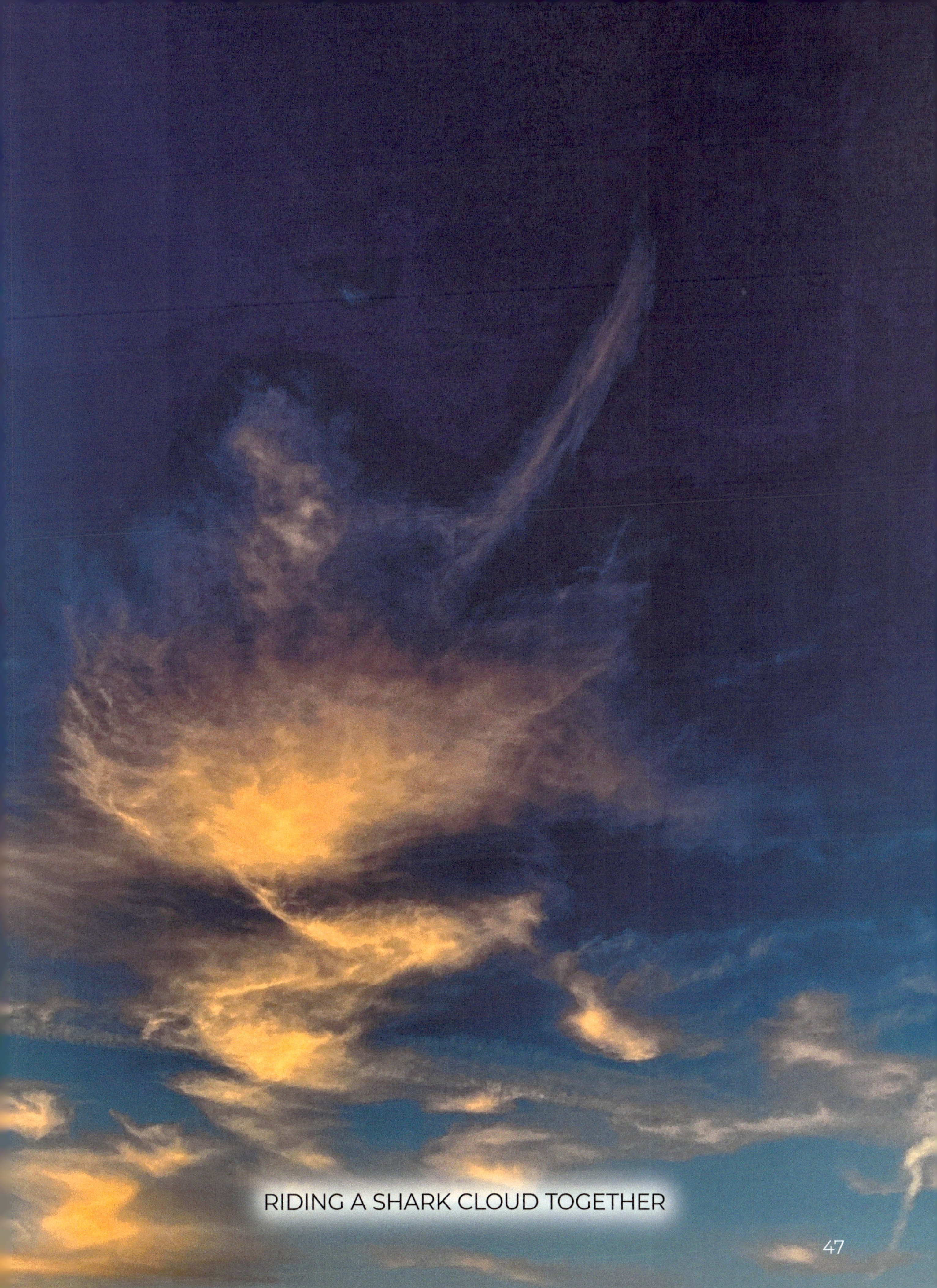
RIDING A SHARK CLOUD TOGETHER

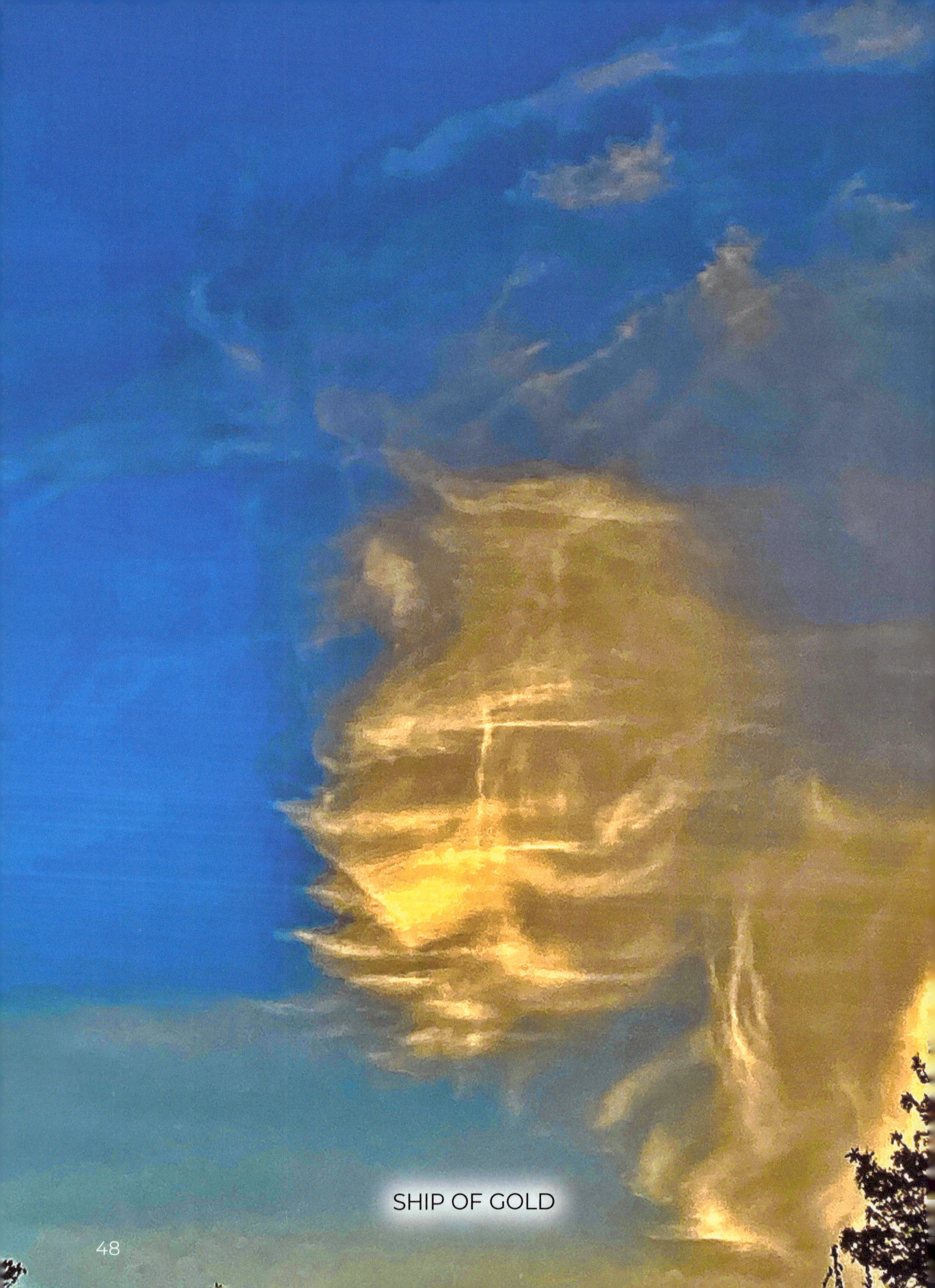

SHIP OF GOLD

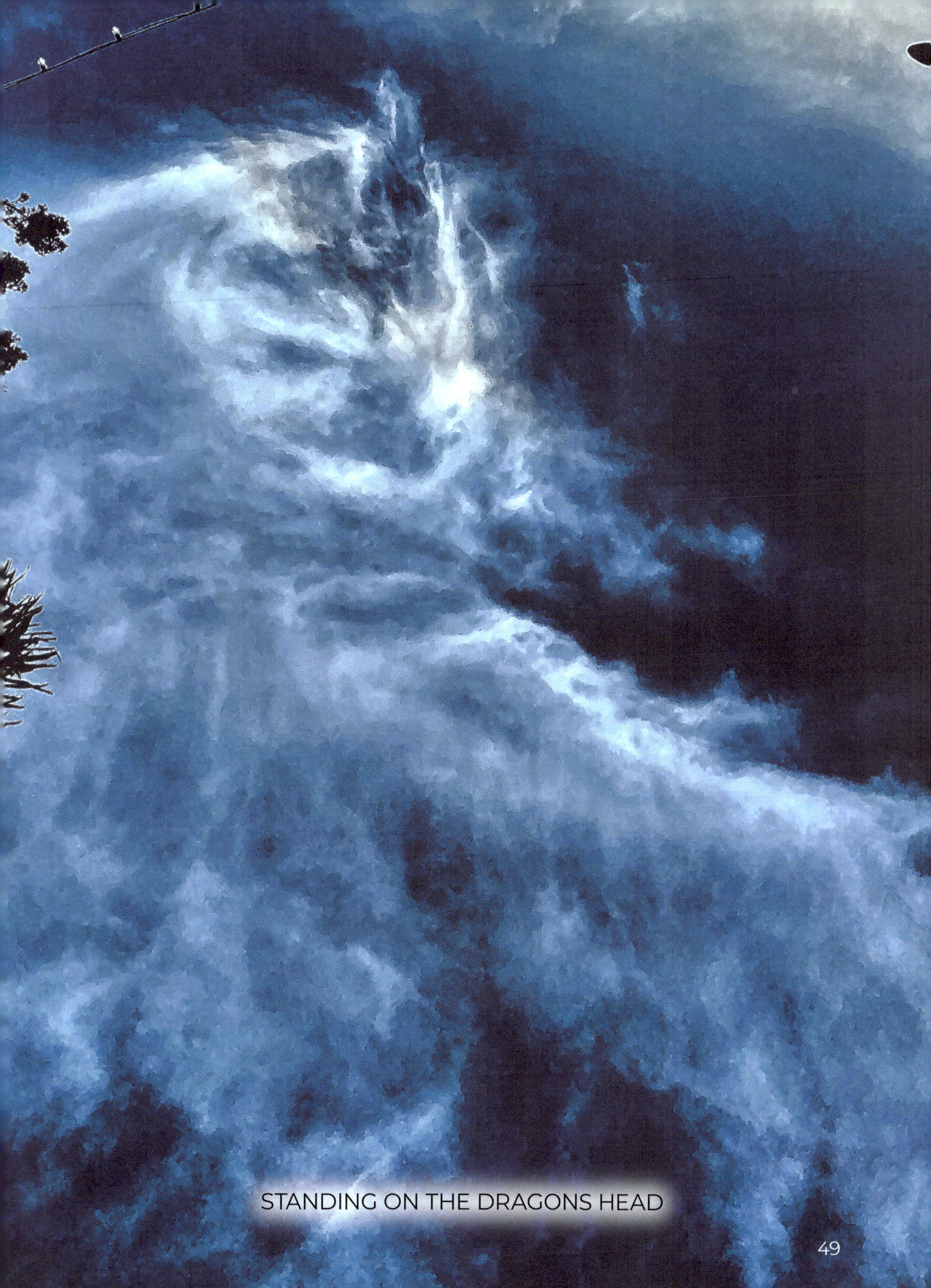
STANDING ON THE DRAGONS HEAD

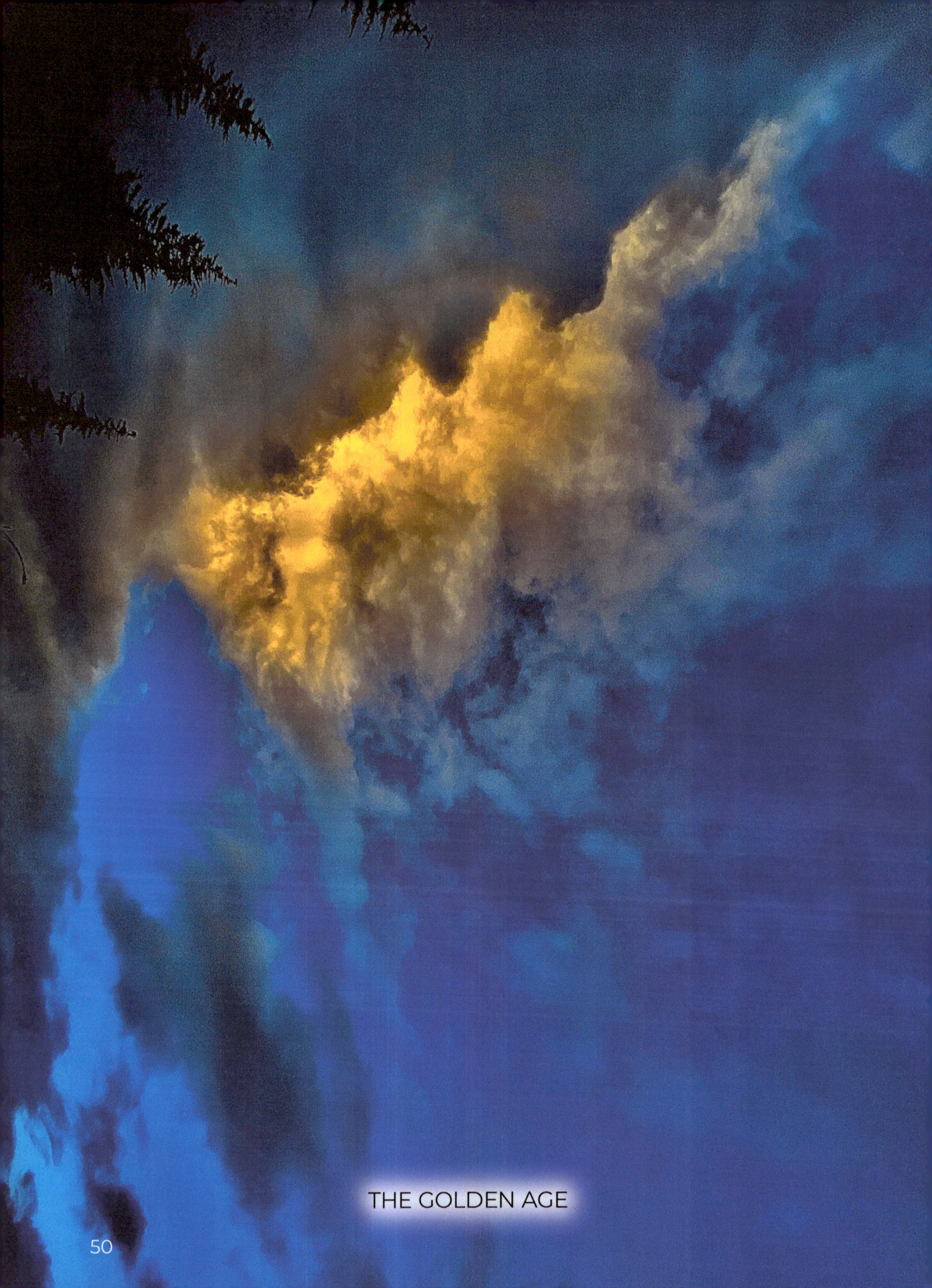

THE GOLDEN AGE

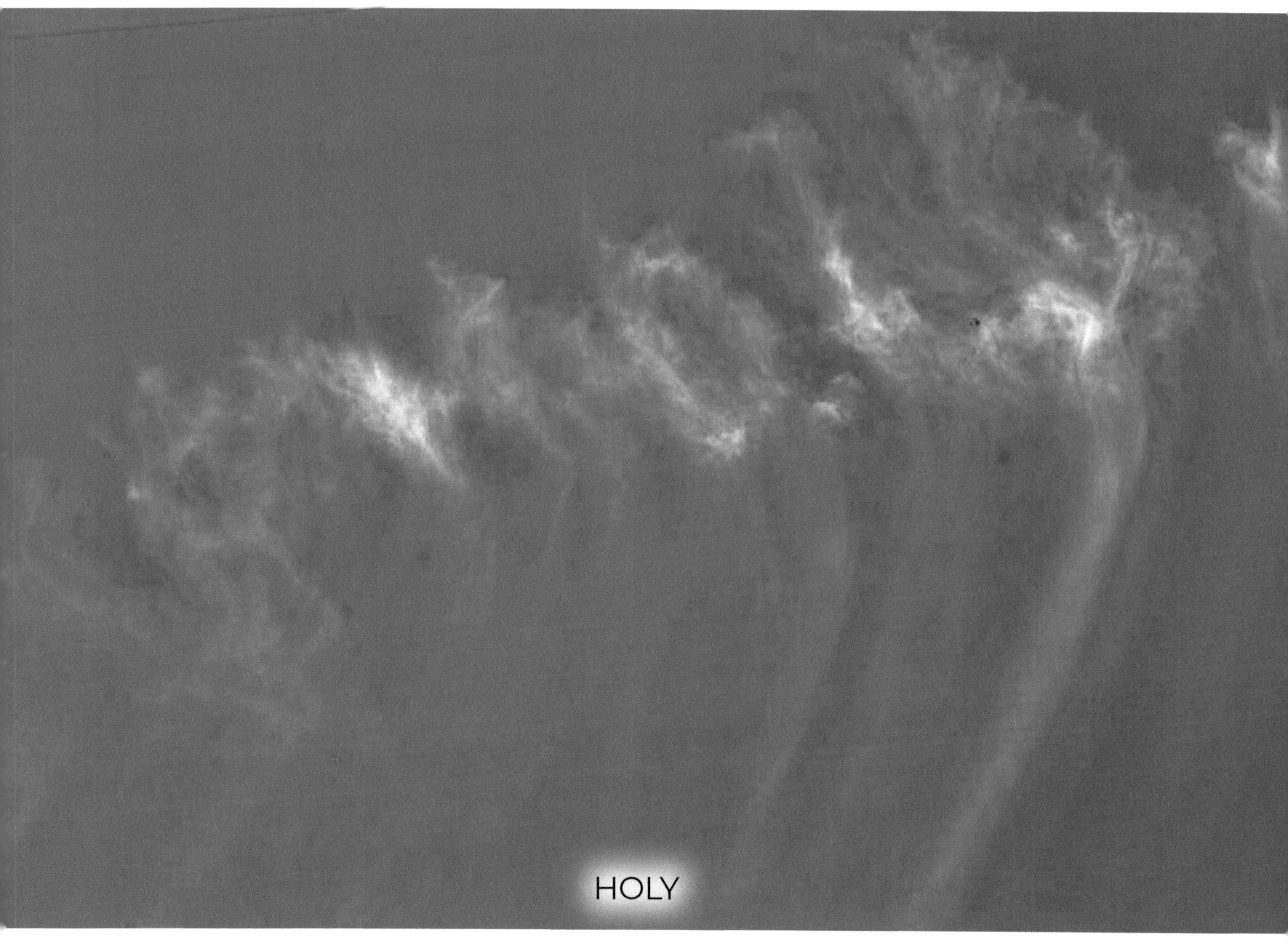
HOLY

About the Author

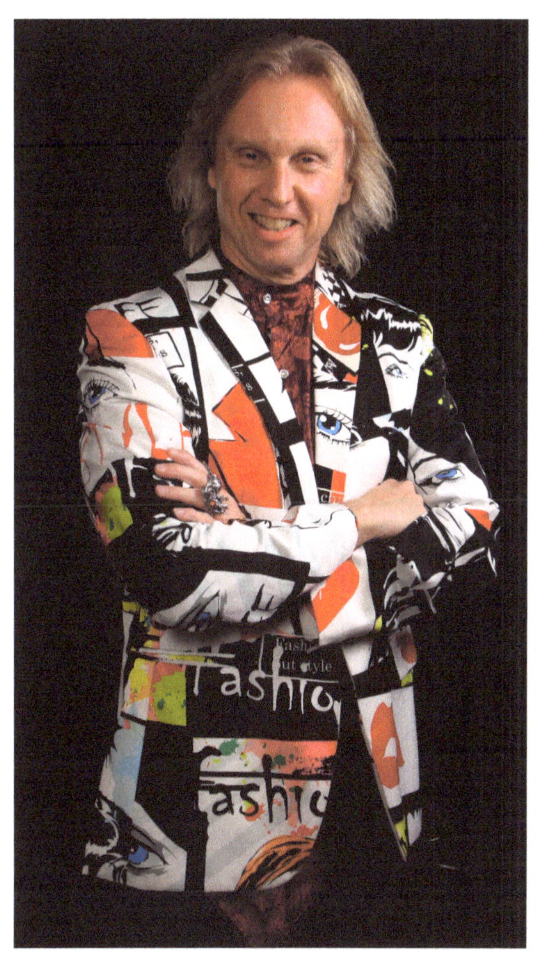

Justyn was born sometime in the last century. He believes that age is just a number and old age only happens if you allow it too. think young, speak young, speak life and not death over yourself and others. The mouth has the power of life and death, so we should use it to create and not to destroy.

He was dropped straight out of heaven and into his mothers womb. Some might even say he landed on his head upon re-entry. If that were not enough at a young age of approximately 6 while riding his bike he flew over the handlebars and landed on his head. Having been knocked unconscious he was carried home by a neighbor friend's parent, Mrs Chambers. the next two days were spent in the hospital with a concussion. A year or two later he would be accidentally hit in the head by a neighbor throwing bricks down the alley. (This may explain why he sees visions, after a few head traumas! JK)

Back in those days he was named John Pratt, by his nine year older brother. Chuck Pratt prayed him into being or existence because he was heavily outnumbered with four sisters. He has two older sisters by the names of Barb and Becky and two younger sisters by the names of Therese and Julie. Justyn is the youngest of the six siblings all born to Rosemary and Charles Pratt. Justyn was told by God to legally change his name, in the spring of 2021. It took him three months to muster the courage to change his name since he knew it was his brother who named him. He knew in his heart that family members would be disappointed or even aggravated by his decision.

But who was he to please, God or man? He chose to be obedient to God and on the day that he went to the court house, upon leaving he photographed a cloud that appeared to be a unicorn in the sky holding a bright and shining diamond upon his outstretched hoof.

Many years prior he was taught by Pastor manuel Ochoa that delayed obedience is disobedience. Justyn is very thankful for the patience of God. God's grace is sufficient for us every day. God grades on the curve of Grace! You see, Justyn had slipped into a deep dark depression after his first born daughter, Linnea Rose died at the age of 26 days. His heart was broken into a million pieces that day. Fifteen years after the death of his first born daughter he would look into the mirror and not recognize himself. He had turned his back on God, his wife Julie Pratt and his three boys Jonathan, David and Noah. their lives had been emotionally turned upside down because their father had chosen selfishness and self centeredness for a time and a season. this situation will be better detailed in the upcoming book "Follow the Signs to your Destiny and Purpose."

The bible says draw close to God and He will draw close to you. That is exactly what Justyn did back in December of 2020. He chose to return to Jesus and ultimately meet God the Father through the love of the Son. The Holy Spirit then began guiding him once more on the journey home, back to his Fathers house. God showed up in his life just in time for him to open his eyes and turn from his wicked ways. Thus becoming a better man, husband, father, brother and friend. The journey home has been one filled with love and laughter as well as sorrow and tears. His heart was being repaired one fragment at a time. Feeling discouraged or sometimes lost on the journey. Justyn would see images first in the air via the clouds, then in the aether. As an avid photographer he began looking up, looking down and looking all around himself. He would then see images in the earth, fire and water. He now has over fifty five thousand images in his collection of The Elements. He has what he refers to as proof of the spirit world working constantly all around us every moment of every day in The Elements. Now two and a half years into the process of drawing close to God, he is healing. Recognizing the darkness within, but choosing the light. Processing the grief, moving through the pain and use of the choices made. He embraced the dark shadows and sat with them for a moment in time. He has learned self love and forgiveness. He has through it all chosen to remain positive, because after all is said and done Positivity is a Super Power! He has leveled up his game and embraced self awareness.

He has chosen obedience to the first and greatest commandment: To love God with your whole heart, mind and soul. The second commandment is to love your neighbor as yourself. God is the artist of Justyn's heart and soul. Justyn is the photographer and artist that God chose to reveal signs and wonders too.

Justyn hopes and prays that you will find peace and love for God, yourself and others on your journey of life.